RAND

Modeling the External Risks of Airports for Policy Analysis

Stephen D. Brady, Richard J. Hillestad

*Supported by the
Netherlands Ministry of Transport,
Public Works and Water Management*

European-American Center for Policy Analysis

Preface

In 1993, RAND/EAC performed a study of the external risk of Schiphol Airport in Amsterdam. That study was motivated by the October 1992 crash of an El Al freight airliner into an apartment building near Amsterdam, killing more than 40 people. The airport was in the midst of an expansion, and the study was commissioned by the Dutch Minister of Transport, Public Works and Water Management to evaluate the changes to external risk that such expansion entailed. The study also evaluated possible mitigating "safety enhancement" measures that might be implemented. Our final report was delivered to the Dutch government in early summer of 1993 (Hillestad et al., 1993).

As part of the evaluation process, it was necessary to develop a computer model to quantitatively estimate various measures of the external safety, such as the risk to individuals living and working in various locations, and the risk of accidents involving large numbers of people on the ground. This model, called Safety Assessment of the Ground Environment of Airports (SAGE-A), was developed as a general tool for the evaluation of airport external risk, and only the input data related it specifically to Schiphol Airport. Furthermore, the model was designed for policy analysis and as such has a large number of "policy levers" represented in the various types of data and parameters used to define an input data set. This generality and policy usefulness have prompted this report describing the need for this type of model and analysis of external airport risk, delineating the specific means used in the model for estimating risk, and finally describing the data available for airport risk analysis and its reduction into parameters needed by the computer model. The report also describes the large number of data uncertainties inherent in a calculation of low-probability risk. Finally, the report describes how the model estimates these uncertainties.

For more information about this model, please contact either of the authors:

RAND
1700 Main Street
Santa Monica, CA 90407
Telephone: 310-393-0411   Fax: 310-393-4818

Requests for information may also be directed to our European Office:

European-American Center for Policy Analysis
TU Delft
Landbergstraat 6
2628 CE Delft
The Netherlands
Telephone: 31-15-78-61-11   Fax: 31-15-78-17-88

Contents

Figures

Tables

Summary

The Need to Evaluate the External Risk of Airports

For airports, an important element of safety is the crash risk to populations living in close proximity. This is called the "external risk" of the airport. It is also called third-party risk because that population is generally an unwilling participant in that risk. Although airports are themselves not usually causal factors in aircraft crashes,[1] most such accidents occur during the landing and takeoff phases of flight, and an airport serves to concentrate that risk on its surrounding population. Despite the improving safety record of commercial aviation over the last decades, there are a number of reasons why it is important to estimate airport external risks quantitatively. The first is airport expansion. Key airports in Western Europe are becoming larger and lie generally in or near major metropolitan areas so that expansion in flight activity often exposes more people on the ground to the risk of an aircraft crash. And, even without expansion of airports, the external risk may be increasing because of the dramatic increase in the number of commercial flights for passengers and freight.[2,3] Increased traffic leads to increased congestion, not only in the air but also on the ground. When congestion interacts with delays caused by weather, the pressures to maintain strict timetables may influence safety.

While airports and airlines in Western Europe undergo expansion and consolidation, the opening of Eastern Europe has increased the number of East-West flights, added new airlines, and forced potentially dangerous interfaces between East-West air control systems, differing aircraft maintenance and training standards, and aircraft of different technological capability. Smaller and less-industrialized countries are not always capable of coping with the requirements for crew training and aircraft maintenance to participate safely in modern air traffic.

---

[1] Airports and Air Traffic Control (ATC) combined have been implicated as a causal factor in only 5 to 7 percent of commercial jet transport accidents. (Douglas Aircraft Safety Data Office, 1991).

[2] European Commission (1991) indicates that the number of air travel passenger movements in Western Europe will rise from 894 million in 1990 to slightly more than 1 billion in 2010. The number of commercial and noncommercial flights using the European airspace will increase from 5.3 million in 1990 to 11.3 million in 2010, an increase of 2.2 times the current 14,500 daily flights.

[3] It is also true that the accident rate in commercial aviation appears to have leveled off in the last decade. This may imply that, as flight operations increase, there will be proportionately more accidents.

Other changes that affect the external safety of airports include the possibility of much larger aircraft (with the likelihood of many more fatalities of passengers and people on the ground if one should crash), deregulation of airlines, and privatization of such functions as ATC.

Safety, then, is an important aspect of the various changes in international aviation in Europe and elsewhere. And an important safety consideration should be the impact of these developments on the innocent bystanders, those people living in the vicinity of airports. Indeed, many environmental impact statements for airports now include an assessment of the third-party risk, and neighborhood groups are becoming increasingly concerned that this risk be properly assessed. External risk assessment should be used to assure all stakeholders that the risks are not increasing substantially and to evaluate various policy options for mitigating the external risk.

This report describes a quantitative model, SAGE-A, designed explicitly for this purpose. This model was used in a major study of Schiphol (Amsterdam) airport to evaluate the external risk as a function of planned expansion and possible safety enhancement measures (Hillestad et al., 1993).

Quantitative Measures of Risk

Two popular measures of third-party risk are *group risk* and *individual risk*. Group risk measures the expected number of fatalities per year caused by aircraft crashes around the airport. Individual risk measures the probability that an individual living or working near an airport will be killed in a given year by an aircraft crash.

A third, slightly less aggregate measure of risk is obtained by grouping individuals in different categories according to their probability of being killed in a given year and then estimating the number of people at risk in each category or interval. Such histograms show the *number of individuals at various levels of risk*, such as the number exposed to a chance of mortality between one in one million and one in ten million per year and the number of individuals exposed to a chance between one in ten million and one in one hundred million per year and so on.

An even more detailed description of external risk is given by *risk contours*, which show on a map the regions and populations near an airport that are subject to given levels of individual risk.

The SAGE-A model described in this report provides outputs of each of these types of external risk measures.

The Role of the Quantitative Analysis

Third-party risk estimates are influenced by a variety of factors, such as aircraft type and related crash rate, whether the aircraft is landing or taking off, and whether the aircraft operation is occurring during business or nonbusiness hours. For example, we can estimate which types of aircraft contribute most to third-party risk. Or we can compare the relative risks during business and nonbusiness hours. If the relative risk is higher during business hours, for instance, it may be because more people are working near the airport (in which case it is important to consider exclusionary safety zoning to incorporate businesses as well as residences) or it may be because of a disproportionate number of flights during those hours. We can determine if particular arrival and departure routes contribute disproportionately to risk. We can estimate whether particular elements of the population are subject to more risk than others.

Risk Assessment for Policy Analysis

Perhaps the most important role of an external risk assessment model is to quantify the effects of various policy alternatives affecting this risk. This in turn means that, in addition to estimating the risk of a particular airport statistically, the model must be amenable to representing a wide variety of policy options affecting and possibly mitigating that risk. These policy options include the following:

- Location and configuration of runways
- Changes in the flight routing for takeoff and landing, as well as stacking areas
- Changes in the use of runways for flight operations
- Changes in the mix of aircraft using the airport and the distribution of takeoffs and landings by aircraft type on various runways
- Changes in the population distribution in the vicinity of the airport. (Such changes may include the locations of businesses and surface transportation corridors near the airport, as well as the day and night variation of this population. They would also include the effect of exclusionary zoning for safety or noise reasons.)

- Factors affecting the possible accident rate of aircraft during takeoff and landing, such as bird control, deicing policies, control of "risky" carriers, etc. (Projected future improvements in aircraft accident rates would be included here as well.)

- Accident mitigation factors, such as emergency response, emergency runways and airports, crash barriers, fire retardant and suppression methods, etc.

The SAGE-A model is specially designed to serve airport policy analysis with respect to these types of changes. It provides the user with input control to simulate the effects of various policy options through data changes and data switches.

The SAGE-A Model

Quantitative estimation of the external risk of airports requires that several types of data be brought together into a probabilistic calculation model appropriate to the specific airport and surrounding community, and that model should also accommodate the many shortcomings and uncertainties in the data available for this estimation. The available data are used to describe the crash probability, the crash location probability, the probability that specific elements of the population are at risk, and the probability of various numbers of fatalities. Section 2 describes the model generally, along with its applicability to the evaluation of policy alternatives that affect airport external risk. Figure S.1 illustrates the various components and outputs of the model.

Detailed Description of the SAGE-A Model

Section 3 of this report provides a detailed description of the mathematical model underlying SAGE-A. The model is based on a Bayesian estimation of the crash rate of flights by specific aircraft types during certain flight phases. The overall crash rate is computed for various flight routings using operational data at a specific airport. This is, in turn, integrated across a population grid to estimate the individual and group risk associated with the airport.

The computer requirements for use of the model are given in Table S.1.

RAND *MR605-S.1*

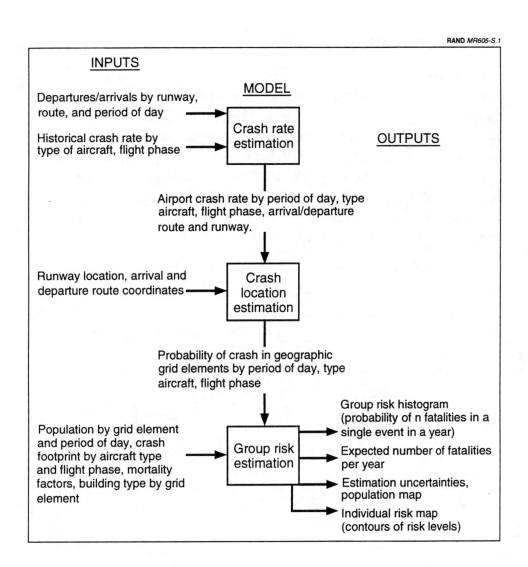

Figure S.1—Overview of the SAGE-A Model

Table S.1

Operational Characteristics of SAGE-A

Programming language	Standard C
Computer memory requirements	10–30 megabytes[a]
Computer running time	1/2 hour on a Sun SPARC-2 workstation[b]
Computing platform	Any computer supporting a C compiler with the requisite RAM

[a]The memory requirement and running time are directly related to the density of the population grid used. Because of the way the model is constructed, it can be tailored to computers with limited memory by sequentially computing the effects on a population grid element of flights from different times, of different types of aircraft, of different flight phases, and using different standard instrument departures (SIDs) and standard terminal arrival routes (STARs).

[b]This is the running time experienced in our own analysis of Schiphol airport external safety, in which we used 100-by-100 m population grid elements over a region 15 by 15 km.

Data Requirements for SAGE-A

SAGE-A uses five basic types of quantitative data: (1) the business- and nonbusiness-hour population distributions around the airport under study, (2) the aircraft operational data (by business and nonbusiness hours, by size of aircraft, and by SID and STAR) at the airport, (3) the aircraft global crash rate data (by mode of flight, size of aircraft, and category of aircraft), (4) the historical global crash location data, and (5) the data describing the impact footprint of a potential crash and mortality rate. Section 4 describes these requirements in detail and provides an illustration of the data reduction techniques used by us in a specific application of the SAGE-A model.

Figure S.2 illustrates schematically the data elements and some data sources.

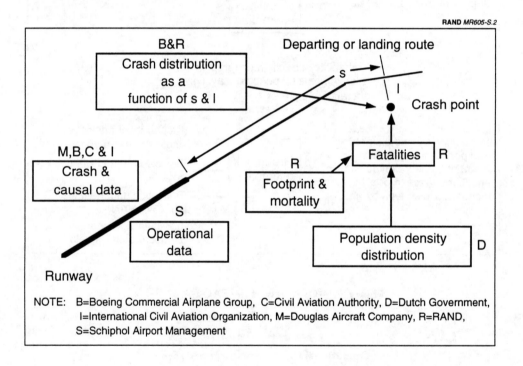

Figure S.2—Airport Data for External Risk Estimation

1. Introduction

The Need to Evaluate the External Risk of Airports

For airports, an important element of safety is the crash risk to populations living in close proximity. This is called the "external risk" of the airport and is considered to be a third-party risk because that population is generally an unwilling participant. Although airports are themselves not usually causal factors in aircraft crashes,[1] most aircraft crashes occur during the landing and takeoff phases of flight, and an airport serves to concentrate that risk on its surrounding population. Despite the improving safety record of commercial aviation over the last decades, there are a number of reasons why it is important to estimate airport external risks quantitatively.

The first is airport expansion. As the twentieth century draws to a close, many key airports in Western Europe are becoming larger. A commonly accepted vision of future transportation includes a limited number of "mainports"—large airports that are also road and rail transportation hubs. For passengers, these mainports will serve as gateways to the hinterland through intermodal feeder lines on transportation corridors. For freight, the air mainports in conjunction with equally centralized maritime ports (such as contemporary Rotterdam) will similarly serve as distribution centers for import and export. Key airports lie generally in or near major metropolitan areas, so that expansion in flight activity often exposes more people on the ground to the risk of an aircraft crash.

The second reason to evaluate external risk is that the number of commercial flights for passengers and freight is increasing dramatically.[2] Increased traffic leads to increased congestion, not only in the air but also on the ground.[3] When congestion interacts with delays caused by weather, the pressures to maintain

---

[1] Airports and air traffic control (ATC) combined have been implicated as a causal factor in only 5–7 percent of commercial jet transport accidents. See Douglas Aircraft (1991).

[2] *The LOTOS Study: A View of Future of Civil Aeronautics* (1991), indicates that the number of air travel passenger movements in Western Europe will rise from 894 million in 1990 to slightly more than 1 billion in 2010. The number of commercial and noncommercial flights using the European airspace will increase from 5.3 million in 1990 to 11.3 million in 2010, an increase of 2.2 times the current 14,500 daily flights.

[3] It is also true that the accident rate in commercial aviation appears to have leveled off in the last decade. This may imply that, as flight operations increase, there will be proportionately more accidents.

strict timetables may influence safety. Improvements in communication, surveillance, and navigation technologies will be used to permit closer spacing between aircraft, increase capacity, and reduce delays at airports and in overburdened air traffic areas. Automation will be used to reduce aircrew workload and to increase aircrew and controller situation awareness. However, increases in traffic and technological sophistication may also lead to increases in pressure on pilots, ground crew, air traffic controllers, dispatchers, and all others who have some responsibility for safety. This increasing production pressure and mental workload could pose additional risks to safety.

Another risk factor is that larger aircraft handling up to 600 passengers have been proposed. The operation of such larger and other smaller but fuller aircraft means that the consequences of an aircraft crash with respect to footprint on the ground and casualties will be more severe, as will be the public reaction to such an event.

The entire international aviation industry is also undergoing rapid changes. Much as air carriers did following deregulation in the United States, some European carriers are merging into multinational companies in response to deregulation, open-skies policies, competition for passengers and freight, and the expected global increase of traffic flow. For example, the Dutch national carrier KLM substantially merged with the American carrier Northwest Airlines. Deregulation, a major driver of the aviation industry, results in cost reduction and tends toward pushing economic margins. As a consequence, economics may dominate safety in decisionmaking. Examples of this might be laxness in maintenance and status monitoring, keeping aged aircraft in the fleet beyond their time,[4] and operating at more than capacity. Although evidence that deregulation has decreased aviation safety is not easily found, Barnett and Higgins argue that there is some confirmation in the experience with U.S. deregulation (Barnett and Higgins, 1989).

While airports and airlines in Western Europe undergo expansion and consolidation, the opening of Eastern Europe has increased the number of East-West flights, added new airlines, and forced potentially dangerous interfaces between Eastern and Western ATC systems, differing aircraft maintenance and training standards, and aircraft of different technological capability. Smaller and less-industrialized countries are not always capable of coping with the requirements for crew training and aircraft maintenance necessary to participate safely in modern air traffic.

---

[4]Some older aircraft will be phased out because they will not be able to meet noise restrictions, however.

Businesses, relying more on air transport, find it more convenient to locate near major airports, increasing the density of daytime workers and surface traffic and, as a consequence, increasing the number of people exposed to risk of an aircraft crash during the period of highest air activity. This is further exacerbated by the desire of individuals to live near their places of work, increasing the population living near the airports.

Safety, then, is an important aspect of the various changes in international aviation in Europe and elsewhere. And an important safety consideration should be the impact of these developments on the innocent bystanders, those people living and working in the vicinity of airports.

In general, even if the crash risk per aircraft flight remains constant, as the number of flight operations expand at an airport, the external risk of the airport to the surrounding population increases. When the crash risk per flight increases, the external risk can also increase, whether or not there is an increase in operations. Factors that militate against increasing external risk include adjustments to takeoff and landing routings, safer flight operations, safer aircraft (or mix of aircraft), and adjustments to population density in the "risky" regions. As physical airport expansion is contemplated or as increases or other changes in operations are considered, the external risk should be measured. Indeed, many environmental impact statements for airports now include an assessment of the third-party risk, and neighborhood groups are becoming increasingly concerned that this risk is properly assessed. External risk assessment should be used to assure all stakeholders that the risks are not increasing substantially and to evaluate various policy options for mitigating the external risk.

This report describes a quantitative model, Safety Assessment for the Ground Environment of Airports (SAGE-A), designed explicitly for this purpose. This model has been used in a major study of Schiphol (Amsterdam) airport to evaluate the external risk as a function of planned expansion and possible safety enhancement measures (see Hillestad et al., 1993).

Third-Party Risks

Various populations may be exposed to a potential harm. Each of the populations exposed may have varying degrees of control over its exposure to the harm. For example, the driver of a car is under direct control of his own safety. His passengers have a lesser degree of control. The driver has willingly volunteered to expose himself to a risk. If he is intoxicated, the passengers can elect not to ride in the car. If an otherwise safe driver has a temporary lapse of performance, the passengers may have relinquished their control. A person sleeping in his bedroom has essentially no control over the fact that a driver could lose control of his car and drive off the road and into the house. Passengers on board an airplane have some control over whether or not they elect to fly. Ground populations have essentially no control over an airplane that crashes into their homes. Populations with little or no control over their exposure are those at **third-party risk.**

Often, those people who have little or no control over the risky situation have not voluntarily accepted the exposure. *Although a primary characteristic of third-party risk is lack of control, a secondary characteristic is often involuntary exposure to the risk.*

Third-party risks associated with transportation can be measured. In automobile accidents, the driver and his passengers are not at third-party risk. The pedestrian hit by a car (excluding, perhaps, pedestrians who elect to jaywalk) is at third-party risk. Third-party group risk (expressed as expected annual fatalities) to a ground population adjacent to airports has been estimated around Los Angeles International Airport as about 0.4 and around Burbank Airport (about 50 km northeast of Los Angeles International Airport) as 0.2 (Solomon et al., 1994).

Third-party risks are an important part of any consideration in the siting of houses, businesses, and other population centers in and around airports. Although the absolute quantitative value of the risk to an individual on the ground is quite small relative to other risks to which he or she is normally exposed, the number of people living near an airport is often large (one or more millions of people within a 25-km radius), and any consequence of an aircraft crash—no matter how unlikely—could affect hundreds of people or more. Hence, any decisions involving the operation of an airport must consider third-party risk.

Quantitative Measures

Two common measures of third-party risk are *group risk* and *individual risk*. Group risk measures the expected number of fatalities per year caused by aircraft crashes around the airport. Individual risk measures the probability that an individual living or working near an airport will be killed in a given year by an aircraft crash.

A third, slightly less aggregate, measure of risk is to group individuals in different categories according to their probability of being killed in a given year and then to estimate the number of people at risk in each category or interval. Such histograms show the *number of individuals at various levels of risk,* such as the number of individuals exposed to a chance of mortality between one in a million and one in ten million per year and the number of individuals exposed to a chance between one in ten million and one in a hundred million per year and so on.

An even more detailed description of external risk is given by *risk contours*, which show on a map the regions and populations near an airport that are subject to given levels of individual risk.

The SAGE-A model described in this report provides outputs of each of these types of external risk measures.

The Role of the Quantitative Analysis

Third-party risk estimates are influenced by a variety of factors, such as aircraft type and the related crash rate, whether the aircraft is landing or taking off, whether the aircraft operation is occurring during business or nonbusiness hours, and so on. For example, we can estimate which types of aircraft contribute most to third-party risk. Or we can compare the relative risks during business and nonbusiness hours. If the relative risk is higher during business hours, for instance, it may be because more people are working near the airport (in which case it is important to consider exclusionary safety zoning to incorporate businesses as well as residences), or it may be because of a disproportionate number of flights during those hours. We can determine whether particular arrival and departure routes contribute disproportionately to risk. If so, it might be possible to consider redesigning those particular routes to avoid overflight of certain populated areas. We can estimate whether particular elements of the population are subject to more risk than others.

A second set of issues involves future operations at the airport. A simple straight-line extrapolation of airport operations growth onto the estimate of third-party risk suggests that the risk would increase in proportion to the operations. However, because the nature of the airline fleet will change in the future—a greater number of larger and probably safer aircraft—it is possible that the risk projection could actually be smaller, or at least less than proportionally as large. Furthermore, the addition of a new runway and certain planned mitigation measures (removing most general aviation from an airport, for example) should reduce the risk still further. Because these features can be represented in a quantitative risk model, we can estimate their effects on third-party risk.

Quantitative risk assessment also puts various options and risks in perspective. Although some flight operations may have a significantly higher crash probability (helicopter flights, for example), if they represent only a small number of operations, then the overall risk to third parties from these operations is not high.[5]

Finally, we would like to compare various safety-enhancement measures in terms of their effect on risk mitigation. For example, if exclusionary safety zoning is used, what is the fractional reduction in third-party risk? If there are certain advances in ATC technology, how might they affect the probability of crash used in the study, and what would the consequent reduction in third-party risk be?

Risk Assessment for Policy Analysis

Perhaps the most important role for a third-party risk assessment model is to quantify the effects of various policy alternatives affecting this risk. This in turn means that, in addition to statistically estimating the risk of a particular airport, the model must be amenable to representing a wide variety of policy options affecting and possibly mitigating that risk. These policy options include the following:

- Location and configuration of runways

- Changes in the flight routing for takeoff and landing, as well as stacking areas

- Changes in the use of runways for flight operations

- Changes in the mix of aircraft using the airport and distribution of takeoffs and landings by aircraft type on various runways

- Changes in the population distribution in the vicinity of the airport. (These may include the locations of businesses and surface transportation corridors near the airport as well as the day and night variation of this population. They would also include the effect of exclusionary zoning for safety or noise reasons.)

- Factors affecting the possible accident rate of aircraft during takeoff and landing, such as bird control, deicing policies, control of "risky" carriers, etc.

---

[5]This does not imply, however, that "dangerous" operations can be accepted if they are sufficiently infrequent. The public has a right to expect a reasonable minimum level of safety for *any* flight.

(Projected future reductions in aircraft accident rate would be included here as well.)

- Accident mitigation factors such as emergency response, emergency runways and airports, crash barriers, fire retardant and suppression methods, etc.

The SAGE-A model is specially designed to serve airport policy analysis with respect to these types of changes. It provides the user with input control to simulate the effects of various policy options through data changes and data switches.

Important Uncertainties Associated with Airport Risk

Risk assessment is as much an art as it is a science. Risk assessments rely on two somewhat distinct methodologies (analytic and empirical) that are used to varying degrees in a particular assessment depending on the nature of the problem and the availability of the data. When nuclear reactor safety is assessed, the analyst typically relies on historical or *empirical* data to learn about the failure rates of individual components in the reactor system. Component failure rates, such as that of a valve or a pipe, are generally well defined. Then these failure rate data are used along with *analytic tools*, such as event trees, to determine the course of events that contribute to an accident and fault trees to determine the reliability of systems. Technologies rich in technical components and well-defined events lend themselves well to risk analyses that rely on both analytic and empirical tools.

However, airport external risk assessment does not evolve from a technology that has a well-defined set of sequences that could lead to an accident. Unlike a nuclear reactor accident, hundreds of variables play a role in determining the likelihood of a plane crash, where the plane crashes, and the effects of that crash. Airport external risk assessment becomes especially difficult when we consider the vast number of uncertainties present in the crash rate data, in the crash distribution, in the consequence assumptions, and in our ability to predict the timeliness and effectiveness of safety enhancement measures.

Uncertainty arises from the facts that aircraft crashes are relatively infrequent and that many factors determine where a plane will crash. So we are dealing with very low probability statistics and wide-ranging consequences. It is therefore necessary to aggregate data among somewhat different historical events.

In summary, the following are the important uncertainties:

- No two accidents are alike, and historical accident data fail to distinguish precisely the causes of past accidents and thus the predictability of future ones. One can address this problem in part by reviewing the applicability of a broad set of past accidents to the airport in question and rule out many of these accidents because they just would not apply.

- Often when the cause of a past accident is determined, the problem is addressed and thus becomes unlikely to happen in the future because of remedial steps taken. So the nature of the accidents in the future will not always be the same as the ones in the past.

- Accidents have many known and unknown causes that contribute to their likelihood, location, and severity. Because of these many variables and infrequent occurrences, inferring characteristics of future accidents from past ones is challenging at best.

- During the course of a policy study, one may want to quantify the effect of taking various safety-enhancement measures. Many of these measures are not quantifiable by their very nature. Others that lend themselves to quantification cannot be quantified in sufficient detail to justify a precise calculation.

Although these uncertainties limit our ability to calculate a precise third-party risk, they do not prevent us from demonstrating general safety trends and some of the relative effects of various policy options. An important feature of the SAGE-A model described in this report is that, in addition to the risk estimates themselves, the model provides measures of the uncertainty of those estimates. The remaining sections of this report describe SAGE-A.

2. SAGE-A: An Overview

The External Risk Estimation Process

Quantitative estimation of an airport's external risk requires that several types of data be brought together into a probabilistic calculation appropriate to the specific airport and its surrounding community while also accommodating the many shortcomings and uncertainties in the data available for this estimation. The available data are used to describe the crash probability, the crash location probability, the probability that specific elements of the population are at risk, and the probability of various numbers of fatalities. In this section, we describe the SAGE-A model generally in terms of the approach to estimating airport external risks, as measured by individual and group risk to individuals living near the airport. We also describe the applicability of the model to the evaluation of policy alternatives that affect airport external risk.

Crash Probability

The probability that a given flight will crash is a function of many uncertain factors and can only be estimated based on historical data adjusted for the airport under study. The worldwide historical data provide a record of the number of previous hull loss crashes (events that result in aircraft loss and are the almost exclusive cause of ground fatalities) by aircraft type. Figure 2.1 illustrates a sample of hull loss accidents in the period between 1959 and 1991. Section 4 describes various sources for these data.

The historical accident rates can also be differentiated by type of carrier, world region, commercial versus private, passenger versus transport, etc. It is important for prediction purposes, however, to maintain some aggregation, say by categorizing aircraft by several size categories and aggregating all carriers and aircraft types into those categories. Too much disaggregation of the data leads to a very sparse set of accidents, which in turn has considerable statistical uncertainty associated with it. The importance of being able to differentiate the accident rate data is that certain accidents can be excluded from the database for a specific airport because they could not have happened there (e.g., accidents due to icing problems in a location that does not have the weather that causes icing). Furthermore, some options for safety improvement include restricting or

10

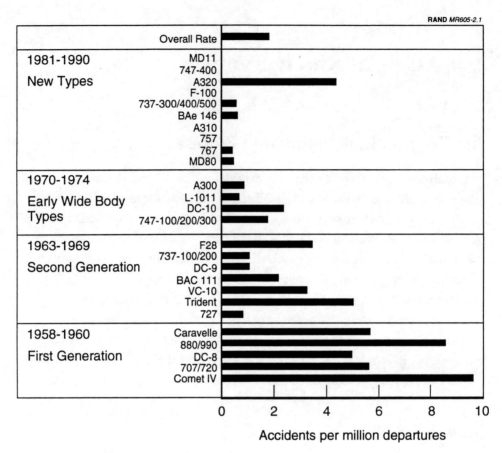

SOURCE: Boeing Aircraft (1991).

Figure 2.1 Hull Loss Accident Rates (excluding sabotage and military action)

eliminating the operations of aircraft types and/or carriers that are more "risky" than others, such as removing general aviation from a main airport. To examine these, it must be possible to affect the crash rate by maintaining a dependence on those categories of aircraft.

The crash rate near a specific airport is also a function of the operational data for the airport and phase of flight. The operational data for an airport include:

- The expected number of takeoffs and landings by type of aircraft, time of day, and day of week

- The expected frequency of use of particular runways by type of aircraft, time of day, and day of week

- The expected frequency of use of particular Standard Instrument Departure routes (SIDs) and Standard Terminal Arrival Routes (STARs) by aircraft type, time of day, and day of week

- Emergency operations data, such as designated emergency runways and other emergency procedures affecting the probability that a flight in trouble lands at that airport, which runway it lands on, and which flight route it would be directed on in preparation for an emergency landing (including fuel dumping areas and procedures).

By combining these operational data with the global crash rate data, it is possible to estimate the expected frequency of hull loss crashes at a specific airport and further estimate the probability that the crash will occur on some arrival or departure route associated with some runway by time of day. The SAGE-A model requires that the crash rate data by aircraft type and the operational data (including specific flight routings and SIDs and STARs) be input separately, and it then determines the expected crash rate to be used in the remainder of the risk estimation. Thus, it is rather an easy matter to examine the effects of flight routing, adjusted frequency of use of runways, new approach and departure patterns, new runways, exclusion or addition of certain types of aircraft, and other operational factors on the external risk of the airport.

The accident rate is also entered to the model as a function of phase of flight. Figure 2.2 illustrates how the historical accident rate is related to flight phase. The figure depicts the percentage of total flight time consumed by each flight phase, the percentage of hull loss accidents occurring in each phase, and the percentage of phase-specific accidents that are fatal. This permits the operational data on takeoffs and landings to be accounted for. We can determine selectively the effects of using particular runways or routes for takeoffs or landings, and we can determine, if there is more of one type of activity than another in a particular period of the day, what the effect will be on the daily dynamics of population near the airport (due to transportation corridors, business hours, etc.).

Crash Location

The next important probability estimated by the SAGE-A model is that of the location of a crash. This is a function of the operational data, the accident rate associated with phase of flight, and the dispersion of accidents with respect to intended flight paths. The first two determine the probability that an accident occurs on some path during takeoff or landing. The latter determines where the crash might occur relative to the path. This is a function of the type of problem leading to the crash, the controllability of the aircraft after a problem occurs, the

12

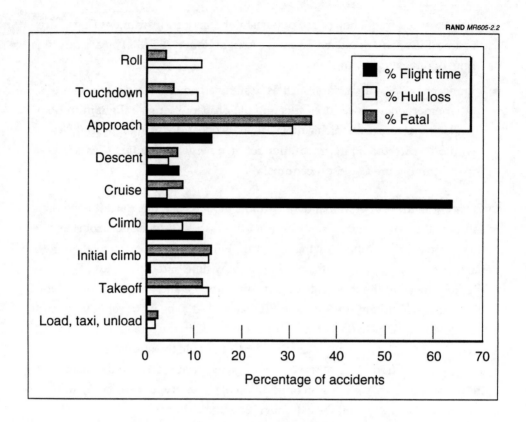

Figure 2.2— Flight Phase of Most Hull Loss Accidents

ability of the pilot to avoid structures or concentrations of people, and the altitude and weather conditions at the time of the incident. One could use an engineering model that specifies the possible glide path and range of dispersion as a function of altitude, the probability of the problem occurring at different distances and altitudes along the flight path, the probability of controllability on the ground and the probability of structure avoidance on the ground. However, as we discuss in Section 4, the data do not support such engineering models very well, both in terms of being able to estimate the requisite probabilities and in terms of historical accident location.

Crews of aircraft in trouble often attempt to fly them back to the airport, and the historical dispersion of crash locations reflects the wide variation in the relative success of these maneuvers. Figure 2.3 shows the distribution of a total of 24 landing (L) and takeoff (T) accident crash sites within 8 km of the end of a runway. The 24 landing and takeoff accident sites are plotted on the basis of reviewing the crash locations of accidents in the vicinity of airports worldwide

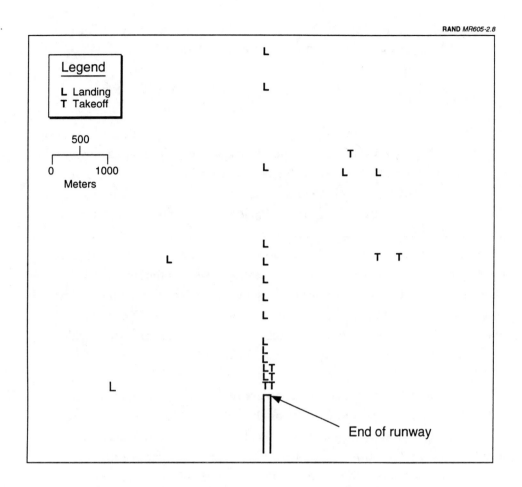

Figure 2.3—Crash Sites Within 8 km of the Runway

and plotting these locations on a single grid.[1] As is described in Section 4, the best statistical model of this crash dispersion is a two-component probability distribution in which one component is the probability of crashing at some position along an extension of the runway centerline and the other component is a uniform probability of crashing somewhere in a rectangular box around the entire runway. The former is dominated by accidents associated with the landing phase.

One other important assumption bears on how to include flight routing information in the crash location estimation. We have generally assumed that the probability distributions described above bend with the SIDs and STARs of

---

[1]Our assessment identified 53 crash locations within 25 km of the end of the runway. Of those 53 crash locations, 24 are located within 8 km of the runway.

14

the departure and arrival routes. It is also possible to assume only straight arrival and departure routes when using the SAGE-A model.

Risk to Individuals

The next step, after the probability of a flight crashing in a specific area has been estimated, is to determine the risk to individuals living in specific areas near the airport. This is done by integrating, for each specific location (a grid cell of arbitrary dimension), the probabilities of crashes in that location from all flights and operations at the airport. Figure 2.4 illustrates this "integration." It depends on the crash footprint, and this is in turn dependent on the probability that a given type of aircraft crashes. The SAGE-A model permits the integration to be done by time of day as well, so that it is possible to predict the risk to individuals at work and at home. These results are best depicted by a map overlaid with contours giving the level of risk to individuals in those zones. The model automatically produces the outputs necessary to create these maps, the grid-based individual risk probability as a function of time period, and the grid location. Figure 2.5 shows a typical risk contour map for one set of calculations for the area near an airport. From these maps, it is possible to see the effect of changing flight routing or runway use on the individual risk in specific regions. SAGE-A also provides aggregate measures of individual risk, the average individual risk in the entire airport area (as a function of time period), and the number of individuals in the airport region who are subject to given levels of risk. The latter output is illustrated in Figure 2.6. Each of these measures can be

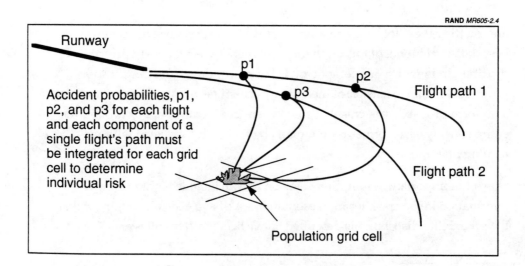

RAND MR605-2.4

Figure 2.4—Integrating the Crash Probabilities to Determine Individual Risk

RAND MR605-2.5

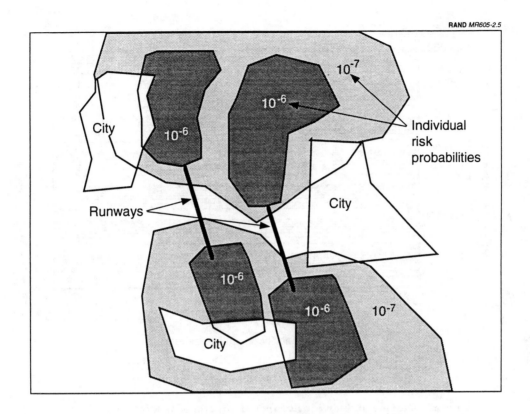

Figure 2.5 —Typical Individual Risk Contour Map

easily used for comparative studies of safety enhancement measures or in examining the impact of airport changes, such as expansion.

Group or Societal Risk

Group risk is a measure of the likelihood of certain numbers of fatalities in accidents. This measure recognizes the importance placed by people on dramatic disasters with larger losses of life compared to a number of accidents with fewer fatalities that may still lead to the same number of overall fatalities.[2] It is a fact of human nature that we are more concerned and aware of tragedies involving many lives lost in a single event than one or a few lives lost over time in many events. The comparison of the relative concern over many traffic fatalities

---

[2]For example, the 1989 Dutch National Environmental Plan proposed a standard for group risk. In that plan, the maximum permissible risk levels for disasters from each industrial activity are as follows: one chance in 100,000 for 10 fatalities or more; one in 10,000,000 for 100 fatalities or more; and so on. *Dutch National Environmental Policy Plan* (1989).

Such standards are more common for fixed facilities involving potentially dangerous activities, such as nuclear power plants and oil refineries. They have not generally been applied to airports.

16

RAND MR605-2.6

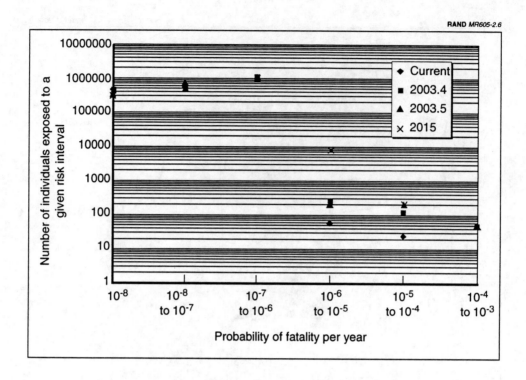

Figure 2.6—Number of Individuals Exposed to Various Risk Intervals During
Business Hours

accumulating to 100 over a short period of time and a single aviation event
causing 100 fatalities illustrates this fact. Because a single aircraft accident is
likely to lead to many deaths, it is important for airports and airlines to
understand the group risk as well as the individual risk of their operations.

Group risk is dependent not only on the crash risk, but on the concentrations of
population in the region near the airport and the mortality probability associated
with a crash, which is a function of types of structures, possible crash barriers,
and emergency response measures. The crash footprint also affects this group
risk and is a function of the types of structures, forestation, crash barriers, type of
aircraft, fuel load (dependent on phase of flight or ability to dump fuel), etc. The
effect of each of these can be represented in the SAGE-A model.

Figure 2.7 shows group risk displayed on a logarithmic scale, the typical way of
depicting such risk. This risk can also be shown as a function of time period and
is affected by the various policy "levers" available to airport management that
can be represented in SAGE-A.

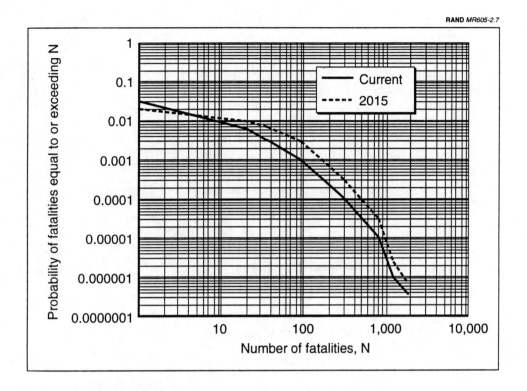

Figure 2.7—Probability of Fatalities Equal to or Exceeding N in a Year

Overview of the Model

Figure 2.8 illustrates the SAGE-A computational elements, as well as the inputs and outputs produced by each. The next section describes the computations in more detail.

18

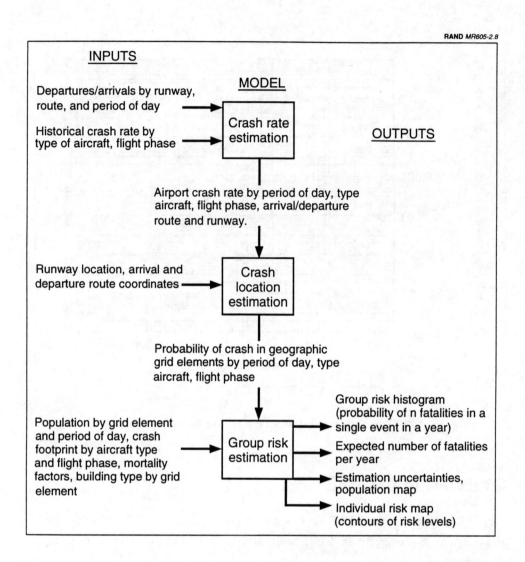

Figure 2.8—Overview of the SAGE-A Model

3. Detailed Model Description

Generality of the Model

The SAGE-A model is designed to be a useful policy-analysis tool for airport external risk and is general—that is, it is not specific to any airport, population area, flight operational data, or policy initiatives. However, it has been developed and implemented with specific consideration for the character and quantity of data available for airport external safety analysis. The aim here is to present the modeling approach itself, along with descriptions of the risk measures obtained by our implementation of the model. Section Four discusses data that have been used in our own application of the model and specifically describes some of the data limitations and uncertainties associated with analysis of airport external risk.

Our model uses standard probabilistic concepts for estimating risk levels for individuals and groups near the airport. Estimates are computed for the likelihood of the crash of a specific flight, a probability distribution for the location of the crash, and the number of third-party fatalities resulting from the crash. To evaluate alternative policies, however, the model also pays specific attention to certain characteristics of each flight—both when interpreting historical data for estimating crash probabilities and when applying these probabilities to anticipated future flight operations at a specific airport. In particular, each flight is characterized by its aircraft type, mode of operation, time of day, assigned runway, and scheduled flight path (SID or STAR) within the airport study area. The occurrence of crash-related events is then conditioned upon these flight attributes in our analysis. Since the overall mix of flights with various characteristics is influenced by airport policies and other factors, this conditioning approach allows us to examine the relative effects of specific scenarios on the safeness of the airport environs.

The Risk-Assessment Model

An individual flight is characterized by its aircraft type, mode, time of day, runway used, and intended route. The model allows any definition of groups of aircraft types, modes, and times of day. However, for specificity, we include in parentheses below the sets of each used in our experiments. Runway and route descriptions and usage patterns are also model inputs of the user's choosing. Further details regarding the definition of the attribute sets, along with runway and route descriptions, are given in Section Four.

Let an individual flight be designated by *amt*, where

$a \in A \equiv$ Set of aircraft types (= {Small, Medium, Large}),
$m \in M \equiv$ Set of operating modes (= {Takeoff/Climb, Landing/Approach}),
$t \in T \equiv$ Set of time periods (= {Business Hours, Nonbusiness Hours}).

There is a probability p_{amt} that an *amt* flight will crash.

A flight will be said to operate "from" a particular runway if it is assigned to the runway for either takeoff or landing operations. Let R be the set of available runways and suppose a particular flight is operated from runway $r \in R$ according to a runway-selection process that may depend upon the flight characteristics a, m, and t. Suppose further that the flight is assigned route (SID or STAR) $q \in Q_r$, where Q_r is the set of routes available for operations from runway r. If the plane crashes, the location of the crash site relative to the assigned route is regarded as stochastic. In particular, a stochastic model is used to determine the location of the crash as measured by its distance s along the route (whether or not the course was strictly followed) and its perpendicular distance l from the route.

For computational purposes, the area surrounding the airport is discretized into a grid of K rectangular cells. When the site of a crash has been selected stochastically, it is mapped into one of the grid cells, indexed by $k \in \{1,2,\ldots,K\}$. The crash kills some number (possibly zero) of people within cell k and its neighboring grid cells. The number of fatalities depends upon the population within the affected cells (which depends upon the time of the crash), as well as upon the size of the impact area and the lethality of the crash (both of which are related to aircraft type and operating mode—determinants of such things as skid distance, destructive force, and explosion potential and magnitude).

For a given year, let λ_{amt} denote the number of flights with the attributes a, m, and t. Since all flights are divided among runways and routes, we have

$$\lambda_{amt} = \sum_{r \in R} \sum_{q \in Q_r} \lambda_{amtqr},$$

where the summand λ_{amtqr} has the obvious interpretation as a refinement of λ_{amt}. These are treated as known quantities, determined by current and projected operational behavior at the airport.

Occurrence of a crash (but certainly not its location) is considered to be independent of a flight's assigned runway and route. Thus, the probability that a given *amtqr* flight crashes remains p_{amt}, from above. Furthermore, all flights are treated as stochastically independent. The number of crashes of *amtqr* flights during the year N_{amtqr} is therefore a binomial random variable with index λ_{amtqr} and probability p_{amt}. Since λ_{amtqr} is large and p_{amt} is small, the binomial distribution of N_{amtqr} can be approximated with a Poisson distribution having mean $\lambda_{amtqr}\, p_{amt}$.

For *amtqr* flights that crash, determination of the crash location is made by drawing from a joint probability distribution of distances s along the route and perpendicular distances l from the route. The distribution of s and l is obtained by fitting a distribution to locations of actual crashes relative to routes (see Section Four). Once the location of the crash has been determined, identifying the grid cell of the crash is straightforward. The computational procedure for determining crash location is described in more detail below.

When a plane crashes at location (grid cell) k, it kills d_{amtk} people. This number of fatalities is naturally regarded as stochastic—that is, d_{amtk} is drawn from some distribution. For reasons discussed below, however, we work with the expected value

$$E(d_{amtk}) = O_{amtk} M_{amtk}\,,$$

where O_{amtk} represents the expected number of people on the ground who are involved in the crash (a function of the population at k during time t, as well as the size, in area, of a typical *amtk* crash) and M_{amtk} is the expected proportion of people involved in the crash who actually lose their lives (mortality factor). Estimation of O_{amtk} and M_{amtk} is detailed below.

We are now prepared to measure the consequences of the crash of a particular flight. If an *amtqr* flight crashes, the assigned runway and route (r and q) help to determine a crash location k. The result is an *amtk* crash with fatalities d_{amtk}. So, the number of people killed if an *amtqr* flight crashes is

$$D_{amtqr} = \sum_{k=1}^{K} I(k\,|\,amtqr)\, d_{amtk}\,,$$

where the indicator function $I(k\,|\,amtqr)$ equals one if the *amtqr* flight crashes in grid cell k and is zero otherwise. Recall that there are N_{amtqr} crashes of *amtqr* flights during a given year. If the number of deaths from the i-th such crash is $D_{amtqr,i}$, then the number of deaths resulting from *amtqr* flights during the year is

$$\sum_{i=1}^{N_{amtqr}} D_{amtqr,i} \quad .$$

(Note that these results can also be derived using compound Poisson methods, with the number of deaths from a crash independent of the crash "arrival" process.) The total number of deaths during the year is then

$$D_T = \sum_{r \in R} \sum_{q \in Q_r} \sum_{t \in T} \sum_{m \in M} \sum_{a \in A} \left(\sum_{i=1}^{N_{amtqr}} D_{amtqr,i} \right) .$$

Computing Estimates of Risk

We now turn our attention to actually computing estimates of the expected total number of fatalities, as well as the expected number of fatalities at each location, or grid cell, during a given year. These are measures of "group risk" that also allow us to estimate the likelihood that an arbitrary person in a particular location will be killed by a crash—that is, the "individual risk."

Distinct differences exist between our efforts to design and implement a computational procedure and our attempts to characterize the underlying stochastic model. The description above highlights the differences in the stochastic and (presumably) deterministic components of the model. Estimating all quantities using proportions gleaned from empirical data blurs this distinction and allows us to rearrange terms in the model in an appealing way—at least from a computational perspective. Sufficient data are not available to supply the model as it is described above. Rather, we must estimate quantities in the model by values derived from a large number of data sources. The number of terms to be manipulated grows significantly, so we shall divide the computations into manageable pieces for our discussion. All estimates required by our computational method are defined below; possible sources of data for each estimate are outlined in Chapter 4.

We wish to estimate (among other measures) the expected total number of fatalities, $E(D_T)$. We have

$$E(D_{amtqr,i}) = E(D_{amtqr})$$

$$= E\left[\sum_{k=1}^{K} I(k \mid amtqr) \, d_{amtk} \right]$$

$$= \sum_{k=1}^{K} P(k \mid C_{amtqr}) \, E(d_{amtk}),$$

where C_{amtqr} is the event that an *amtqr* flight crashes and $P(k|C_{amtqr})$ is the estimated probability that such a crash will be located at cell k. Therefore, we have

$$E(D_T) = \sum_{r\in R} \sum_{q\in Q_r} \sum_{t\in T} \sum_{m\in M} \sum_{a\in A} \lambda_{amtqr}\, p_{amt}\, E(D_{amtqr,i})$$

$$= \sum_{r\in R} \sum_{q\in Q_r} \sum_{t\in T} \sum_{m\in M} \sum_{a\in A} \left[\lambda_{amtqr}\, p_{amt} \sum_{k=1}^{K} P(k|C_{amtqr})\, E(d_{amtk}) \right]$$

$$= \sum_{k=1}^{K} \sum_{t\in T} \sum_{m\in M} \sum_{a\in A} \left[E(d_{amtk}) \sum_{r\in R} \sum_{q\in Q_r} \lambda_{amtqr}\, p_{amt}\, P(k|C_{amtqr}) \right]$$

$$= \sum_{k=1}^{K} \sum_{t\in T} \sum_{m\in M} \sum_{a\in A} E(D_{amtk}),$$

where $E(D_{amtk})$ is the expected number of fatalities during the year (group risk) at location k caused by crashes of flights with the characteristics a, m, and t. This formulation allows us to identify by location the comparative levels of risk around the airport. Moreover, by computing the values $E(D_{amtk})$ for all a, m, t, and k, we can build a large collection of aggregate risk measures through manipulation of the summations shown above. For example, the measure

$$E(D_k) = \sum_{t\in T} \sum_{m\in M} \sum_{a\in A} E(D_{amtk})$$

gives the expected number of fatalities at location k caused by all crashes during the year. The measure

$$E(D_a) = \sum_{k=1}^{K} \sum_{t\in T} \sum_{m\in M} E(D_{amtk})$$

gives the expected number of fatalities during the year caused by all crashes of aircraft of type a, regardless of crash location, whereas

$$E(D_{ak}) = \sum_{t\in T} \sum_{m\in M} E(D_{amtk})$$

allows a location-specific comparison of aircraft types. Additional aggregate risk measures can be built in a similar fashion. Our selection of risk-measure outputs are described in later paragraphs. Here, we shall focus on the computation of the building block

$$E(D_{amtk}) = E(d_{amtk}) \sum_{r\in R} \sum_{q\in Q_r} \lambda_{amtqr}\, p_{amt}\, P(k|C_{amtqr}).$$

The formula for $E(D_{amtk})$ is the product of two principal components. The first component, $E(d_{amtk})$, is the expected number of fatalities from any *amtk* crash. The remaining (double summation) component is the expected number of *amtk* crashes. The summand focuses on crashes from a particular runway and with a particular assigned route. The term $\lambda_{amtqr}\, p_{amt}$ yields the total number of *amt* crashes for the runway and route—that is, the number of *amtqr* crashes. $P(k|C_{amtqr})$ apportions these crashes among the grid-cell locations. We shall discuss the individual terms from the formula for $E(D_{amtk})$ in the following order: λ_{amtqr}, p_{amt}, $E(d_{amtk})$, and $P(k|C_{amtqr})$.

We estimate the total number of *amtqr* flights for a given year with

$$\lambda_{amtqr} \cong E(O_T)\,P(q|q \in Q_r, r, amt)\,P(r|amt)\,P(amt),$$

where $P(amt)$ is the proportion of all local flights that have characteristics a, m, and t; $P(r|amt)$ is the proportion of *amt* flights that use runway r; $P(q|q \in Q_r, r, amt)$ is the proportion of *amt* flights from runway r that are assigned route $q \in Q_r$; and O_T is the number of operations (flights) of all types during the year. $P(amt)$, in turn, is defined by the conditioning rule

$$P(amt) = P(a|mt)\,P(m|t)\,P(t),$$

with $P(t)$ equal to the proportion of local operations that occur during time period t; $P(m|t)$, the proportion of flights during time t that operate in mode m; and $P(a|mt)$, the proportion of such operations that are conducted by aircraft of type a.

Note that the above quantities can be obtained from current and projected operational information for an airport. For example, $P(t)$ comes from the airport's records of distribution of flights by time of day. For some terms, reasonable independence assumptions allow us to relax some conditions. For instance, if aircraft passing through an airport land and take off during the same general time of day, $P(a|mt)$ can be replaced in our analysis by $P(a|t)$, ignoring the operational mode. Similarly, the time period can be ignored for assignment of runways and routes, weakening the conditions in $P(r|amt)$ and $P(q|q \in Q_r, r, amt)$. These simplifications merely represent special cases of the problem, however. They can be accommodated with the above formulas exactly as written, although many proportions would be unnecessarily repeated across conditions that might be judged irrelevant in the data. For efficiency, our model implementation takes account of these modifications when desirable. The expected flight operational level, $E(T)$, is varied among computational runs for scenarios involving different years. As noted, Section 4 details how the data are used to represent these quantities.

The crash probability p_{amt} is a central driving force for the model—and perhaps the most intriguing value to estimate. The estimation of the probability of the occurrence of a crash with particular characteristics during an arbitrary flight operation requires intensive data-preparation efforts. Care must be taken in using *historical* accident data to predict *future* accidents. The probability that a certain type of crash will occur must be derived from information about known crashes, but *it must also account for the fact that such crash data represent only a small portion of all flight operations*. Bayesian analysis provides the mechanism for doing this, but it requires that existing crash data be examined in a particular way. An additional concern stems from the fact that a particular airport might not have sufficient local crash data for predicting future accidents, requiring the use of *global* data for estimating the likelihood of a *local* crash. Appropriate assumptions regarding similarities between the world's airports and the airport under study must be made, with corresponding screening of accident data that violate these assumptions (for example, accidents influenced by mountainous terrain should be removed from the data when a low-lying airport is being studied—or aggregate, marginal data should be properly treated by conditioning on terrain conditions).

The use of appropriately screened global data to estimate p_{amt} for a specific airport prompts us to enhance our notation slightly. In the following, all terms subscripted with w refer to global (worldwide) values. We have

$$p_{amt} = \text{probability a local } amt \text{ flight will crash}$$

$$\cong \text{probability a global } amt \text{ flight will crash}$$

$$= p_{w,amt}$$

$$\cong \frac{P_w(amt \mid C)\,P_w(C)}{P_w(amt)} \quad \text{(Estimate with proportions and Bayes rule)}$$

$$= \frac{P_w(amt \mid C)\,P_w(C)}{P_w(a)P_w(m)P_w(t)},$$

where the last identity assumes independence (at the cumulative worldwide level) of aircraft type, mode, and time of flight. Here, C indicates that a crash occurs, $P_w(C)$ is the proportion of relevant global operations resulting in a crash near the airport, and $P_w(amt \mid C)$ is the proportion of known crashes that have flight characteristics a, m, and t. $P_w(a)$, $P_w(m)$, and $P_w(t)$ are, respectively, the proportion of global operations flown by aircraft of type a, the proportion flown in mode m, and the proportion flown during time period t.

As noted above, $E(d_{amtk})$, the expected number of fatalities from an *amtk* crash, is the product of two components:

$$E(d_{amtk}) = O_{amtk}M_{amtk}.$$

We estimate O_{amtk}, the expected number of people on the ground who are involved in the crash, using

$$O_{amtk} = E(P_{tk}) \frac{E(Z|C_{amtk})}{A_k},$$

where P_{tk} is the population at location k during time period t, Z is the size (area) of the crash impact zone, and A_k, $A_k \leq Z$, is the area of grid cell k. (In our analysis, we use square, equally sized grid cells, so A_k is identical for all k.) Expected crash size, $E(Z|C_{amtk})$, is estimated with average impact areas (from historical data) for each combination of aircraft type and flight mode only. (Location and time are not considered significant compared to aircraft size and fuel load—as determined by operational mode.) Note that the formula estimates the number of fatalities as a multiple (which can be greater than one) of the expected population in the grid cell considered to be the center of the crash. More-elaborate numerical techniques for spreading the crash effects to portions of the neighboring cells can be devised. However, the character of the available population data has not supported such an effort for our purposes.

The mortality factor M_{amtk} is estimated using historical average fractions of people in the impact zone of a crash who actually die. Although not required by the model, mortality factors in our study are identical across time periods and locations.

Finally, we describe the estimation of the locational crash probabilities $P(k|C_{amtqr})$. Although the aircraft type, mode, and time period influence the choice of runway and route—as provided by the conditional components of λ_{amtqr}—it is reasonable to assume that these factors (and even the runway) do not further influence the crash location, once the intended route has been chosen. That is,

$$P(k|C_{amtqr}) = P(k|C_q),$$

where C_q indicates the crash of a flight operation assigned to route $q \in Q_r$. The quantity $P(k|C_q)$ is computable using only a route description, along with a distribution of crash sites about intended routes.

Suppose that the crash occurs at a point c and that route q can be described by a set of n piecewise linear segments. Mathematically, the v-th route segment is represented by the line segment from x^{v-1} to x^v, with x^0 representing the start of the route (the takeoff or touchdown point) and x^n representing a point along the route beyond the boundary of the airport study area. Suppose that empirical data on crash location (see Section 4) have been used to estimate the bivariate density function $f(s,l)$, where the pair (s,l) provides coordinates of the crash site according to the following scheme: The coordinate l is the orthogonal distance from the crash site to the nearest segment of q—if such an orthogonal projection exists. When an orthogonal projection to a segment of q does not exist (true for all points c in a cone extending from each joint in the segmented route), l is the minimum distance from the crash site to a line-segment endpoint $x^0, x^1, ..., x^n$. That is,

$$l = \min\left\{\min_{v \in N} \|c - \omega^v\|, \min_{v=0,1,...,n} \|c - x^v\|\right\},$$

where $\|\cdot\|$ is the Euclidean norm, ω^v is the orthogonal projection of c onto the *line* containing the line segment $\left[x^{v-1}, x^v\right]$, and

$$N = \left\{v \mid v = 1, 2, ..., n; \; \omega^v \in \left[x^{v-1}, x^v\right]\right\}.$$

(The condition on ω^v permits only those projections that fall on actual flight segments—not merely along extended lines containing flight segments.) Ties are broken by choosing the lowest index v. The coordinate s is the distance from x^0 to the point along q chosen in the minimization above.

The procedure used for estimating $P(k|C_q)$ identifies the centerpoint c^k of grid cell k, determines its coordinates s^k and l^k using the above procedure, and estimates the probability by multiplying $f(s^k, l^k)$ by the area A_k. Following this computation for all $k \in \{1, 2, ..., K\}$, each individual product is divided by the total probability assigned to the grid so that the probabilities sum to one. (This normalization step allows us to use $A_k = 1$, thus avoiding the multiplication above, when all grid cells are equally sized.)

Output Measures of the Model

Most output measures are built using the computed locational fatality estimates $E(D_{amtk})$. However, the basic model is also used to extract additional useful quantities during a run.

The principal risk measures are variations of group risk and individual risk. Group risk is the expected number of fatalities, aggregated in a number of ways, as described above. Individual risk is computed by dividing certain group risks by the number of individuals exposed to that group risk. In particular, if the expected fatalities at location k during time period t is $E(D_{tk})$, as defined above, then each individual has an expected likelihood (individual risk) of $E(D_{tk})/E(P_{tk})$

of dying from an airplane crash during the year. Obviously, individual risks are only computed per time period because of their reliance on population values.

The following risk measures are included in the selected outputs of our risk-model implementation. All measures are aggregated over all aircraft types and modes:

Expected number of fatalities (group risk) for each time period and location,

$$E(D_{tk}) = \sum_{m \in M} \sum_{a \in A} E(D_{amtk});$$

expected number of fatalities (group risk) for each time period aggregated over all locations,

$$E(D_t) = \sum_{k=1}^{K} \sum_{m \in M} \sum_{a \in A} E(D_{amtk});$$

expected number of fatalities (group risk) for each location aggregated over all time periods,

$$E(D_k) = \sum_{t \in T} \sum_{m \in M} \sum_{a \in A} E(D_{amtk});$$

expected number of fatalities (group risk) aggregated over all time periods and locations,

$$E(D_T) = \sum_{k=1}^{K} \sum_{t \in T} \sum_{m \in M} \sum_{a \in A} E(D_{amtk});$$

expected square of number of fatalities (squared group risk) for each time period aggregated over all locations,

$$E(D_t^2) = \sum_{k=1}^{K} \sum_{m \in M} \sum_{a \in A} E(D_{amtk}^2);$$

expected square of number of fatalities (squared group risk) aggregated over all time periods and locations,

$$E(D_T^2) = \sum_{k=1}^{K} \sum_{t \in T} \sum_{m \in M} \sum_{a \in A} E(D_{amtk}^2);$$

individual risk for each location and time period,

$$E(D_{tk})/E(P_{tk});$$

and estimates of the probability of having m, $m = 1, 2, \ldots$, or more people killed in a single crash during the year.

Additional descriptive output includes:

- Population summary by time period and location, including total expected population, location and value of maximum expected population, and population histogram with user-specified histogram levels

- Group-risk summary by time period and aggregated over all time periods, including location and value of maximum group risk, and group-risk histogram with user-specified histogram levels

- Individual-risk summary by time period, including population, location, and value of maximum individual risk, and individual-risk histogram with user-specified histogram levels.

Finally, variance estimates are reported to quantify the uncertainty in the risk measures by time period and aggregated for all time periods. The estimation of uncertainty as described by these variance estimates is described next.

How the Model Treats Uncertainties

Many of the quantities required by the model above are not directly available. We therefore must supply numerous quantities for estimating the various model components. For example, the number of *amtqr* flights during a year, λ_{amtqr}, is computed using estimates of total flight operations, along with the estimated proportion of all flights that have attributes a, m, and t, the proportion of *amt* flights that use runway r and the proportion of such flights that subsequently use route $q \in Q_r$. These quantities introduce uncertainty into our computations, although the model treats them as if they are known.

Two quantities are modeled stochastically. These are N_{amtqr}, the number of crashes of *amtqr* flights during the year, and k, the location of a crash, if one occurs. As discussed above, the number of crashes is assumed to have a Poisson distribution, given λ_{amtqr} and p_{amt}, and the location of a crash is determined by drawing from the distribution of s and l. The parameters that determine this latter probability distribution are modeled as if they are fixed and known; however, they are actually estimated (with uncertainty) from data on previous crashes.[1] This provides another source of uncertainty, albeit one that has a

---

[1]RAND's representation of crash location is not mechanistic. Instead, distributions were fitted to the prominent features of the data. The most prominent features were the clustering of crashes on the extended runway centerline and the differences between crashes on and off the centerline. Crashes on the centerline tended to be much closer to the end of the runway than were crashes off the centerline. Also, crashes on the centerline had (by definition) no dispersion about the centerline, whereas crashes off the centerline had a substantial dispersion. These qualitative features were true of takeoff and landing crashes, and formal statistical tests gave no indication that different

somewhat different flavor than does uncertainty about the number and location of crashes. As described in Section 4, we must also estimate the probability p_{amt} using proportions of previous crashes with certain characteristics.

Finally, there is an uncertain quantity—one that would be modeled naturally as stochastic if enough were known to do so: d_{amtk}, the number of third-party deaths if a crash occurs in grid cell k. Our attempts to model third-party deaths in detail would be compromised by the lack of sufficient available data and historical studies of the phenomena associated with third-party deaths in air crashes. Therefore, we assess only the expected number of third-party deaths via O_{amtk} and M_{amtk} above and treat the uncertainty qualitatively.

In our analysis, we take account of uncertainty from three sources: the number of crashes; the location of a crash, if one occurs; and the uncertainty arising from having estimated p_{amt}, the probability of the crash of an *amt* flight. We use a quantitative measure of uncertainty, the so-called *predictive variance*, derived by combining the uncertainty arising from these three sources.

The predictive variance is most naturally defined using Bayesian terminology: It is the variance of the unconditional probability distribution for the (unknown) quantity in question—in our case, the number of fatalities in a given year. The term "unconditional" indicates that the distribution is not conditional on unknown parameters—in our case, the p_{amt}. The unconditional distribution for deaths in a given year would be obtained by specifying the conditional distribution for deaths—described by the stochastic model above—and computing the integral of that distribution with respect to the posterior distribution of the unknown parameters in the stochastic model.

It would be ideal to represent uncertainty using a full probability distribution. However, given the limitations of the data and the difficulty of working with full distributions, we choose to use variance as a measure of uncertainty. Thus, we avoid specifying all the relevant distributions beyond the first two moments.

We want the predictive variance of

$$D_T = \sum_{r \in R} \sum_{q \in Q_r} \sum_{t \in T} \sum_{m \in M} \sum_{a \in A} \left(\sum_{i=1}^{N_{amtqr}} D_{amtqr,i} \right).$$

---

distributions should be used for takeoff and landing, although for a sample as small as our takeoff sample, the power of such tests is low.

For the moment, treat the p_{amt} as known. We need to derive $E(D_T|\mathbf{p})$ and $Var(D_T|\mathbf{p})$, where $\mathbf{p}$ is a vector formed from the p_{amt}. In the sequel, we drop the notation "$|\mathbf{p}$" for simplicity. Now,

$$E(D_T) = \sum_{r \in R} \sum_{q \in Q_r} \sum_{t \in T} \sum_{m \in M} \sum_{a \in A} E(N_{amtqr}) E(D_{amtqr,i})$$

$$= \sum_{r \in R} \sum_{q \in Q_r} \sum_{t \in T} \sum_{m \in M} \sum_{a \in A} \lambda_{amtqr} \, p_{amt} \, E(D_{amtqr,i}).$$

The first equality follows from the presumed independence of the stochastic process that generates crashes and the process that generates deaths given that a crash has occurred. The second equality follows because N_{amtqr} is Poisson with mean $\lambda_{amtqr} \, p_{amt}$. Invoking a standard conditioning decomposition for variances, we obtain

$$Var(D_T) = E(Var(D_T|\mathbf{N})) + Var(E(D_T|\mathbf{N})),$$

where $\mathbf{N}$ is a vector formed from the N_{amtqr}. But, since

$$Var(D_T|\mathbf{N}) = \sum_{r \in R} \sum_{q \in Q_r} \sum_{t \in T} \sum_{m \in M} \sum_{a \in A} N_{amtqr} \, Var(D_{amtqr})$$

and

$$E(D_T|\mathbf{N}) = \sum_{r \in R} \sum_{q \in Q_r} \sum_{t \in T} \sum_{m \in M} \sum_{a \in A} N_{amtqr} \, E(D_{amtqr}),$$

we have

$$Var(D_T) = \sum_{r \in R} \sum_{q \in Q_r} \sum_{t \in T} \sum_{m \in M} \sum_{a \in A} \lambda_{amtqr} \, p_{amt} \, Var(D_{amtqr})$$

$$+ \sum_{r \in R} \sum_{q \in Q_r} \sum_{t \in T} \sum_{m \in M} \sum_{a \in A} \lambda_{amtqr} \, p_{amt} \, E(D_{amtqr})^2$$

$$= \sum_{r \in R} \sum_{q \in Q_r} \sum_{t \in T} \sum_{m \in M} \sum_{a \in A} \lambda_{amtqr} \, p_{amt} \, E(D_{amtqr}^2).$$

The p_{amt} have been treated as known in deriving $E(D_T|\mathbf{p})$ and $Var(D_T|\mathbf{p})$. Since they are not known, however, we have (using Bayesian terminology) a joint distribution for the vector $\mathbf{p}$. More specifically, we have a mean vector $E(\mathbf{p})$ and a covariance matrix $Cov(\mathbf{p}) = \Gamma$. Using the standard decomposition

$$Var(D_T) = E(Var(D_T|\mathbf{p})) + Var(E(D_T|\mathbf{p})),$$

we obtain

$$\text{Var}(D_T) = \sum_{r \in R} \sum_{q \in Q_r} \sum_{t \in T} \sum_{m \in M} \sum_{a \in A} \lambda_{amtqr} \, \text{E}(p_{amt}) \, \text{E}(D^2_{amtqr})$$

$$+ \text{Var}\left(\sum_{t \in T} \sum_{m \in M} \sum_{a \in A} p_{amt} \, \Delta_{amt} \right),$$

where

$$\Delta_{amt} = \sum_{r \in R} \sum_{q \in Q_r} \lambda_{amtqr} \, \text{E}(D_{amtqr}).$$

If the Δ_{amt} are used to form a vector Δ, with ordering of components consistent with that of $\mathbf{p}$, then

$$\text{Var}(D_T) = \sum_{r \in R} \sum_{q \in Q_r} \sum_{t \in T} \sum_{m \in M} \sum_{a \in A} \lambda_{amtqr} \, \text{E}(p_{amt}) \, \text{E}(D^2_{amtqr}) + \Delta^T \Gamma \Delta,$$

where the superscript T indicates matrix transposition.

Finally, variance estimates are reported to quantify the uncertainty in the group-risk measures by time period and aggregated for all time periods. These are the incidental variance, in which route-choice, crash, and damage estimates are assumed known,

$$\text{E}(D^2_t) - \left[\text{E}(D_t) \right]^2 \quad \text{and} \quad \text{E}(D^2_T) - \left[\text{E}(D_T) \right]^2.$$

Our use of variances and standard deviation is limited, since little can be determined about the underlying distribution of group risk. However, we can invoke Chebyshev's inequality in the usual way to make statements about the likelihood of experiencing real fatality levels beyond a certain range of values.

Operational Aspects of the SAGE-A Model

We conclude this section with Table 3.1, which describes the computer requirements and other characteristics of the model.

Table 3.1

Operational Characteristics of SAGE-A

Programming language	Standard C
Computer memory requirements	10–30 megabytes[a]
Computer running time	1/2 hour on a Sun SPARC-2 workstation[b]
Computing platform	Any computer supporting a C compiler with the requisite RAM

[a]The memory requirement and running time are directly related to the density of the population grid used. Because of the way the model is constructed, it can be tailored to computers with limited memory by sequentially computing the effects on a population grid element of flights from different times, of different types of aircraft, of different flight phases, and using different SIDs and STARs.

[b]This is the running time experienced in our own analysis of Schiphol airport external safety, in which we used 100-by-100 m population grid elements over a region 15 by 15 km.

4. Data Requirements for the Risk-Assessment Model

Overview of the Data Requirements

SAGE-A uses five basic types of quantitative data: (1) the business- and nonbusiness-hour population distributions around the airport under study, (2) the aircraft operational data (by business and nonbusiness hours, size of aircraft, and SID and STAR) at the airport, (3) the aircraft global crash rate data (by mode of flight, size of aircraft, and category of aircraft), (4) the historical global crash location data, and (5) the data describing the impact footprint of a potential crash and mortality rate. Figure 4.1 illustrates schematically the data elements and some data sources.

To estimate the third-party risk for a given year, we consider the total number of aircraft movements at the specific airport in that year. We then classify the movements by aircraft type,[1] flight mode (takeoff or landing), runway used, SID or STAR, and business or nonbusiness hours.

Next, one must assemble the global hull loss accident rates for the types of aircraft used at the airport.[2] Hull loss data are used because they are the most relevant to the third-party external safety calculations. Only a negligible number of accidents have caused third-party fatalities outside the airport that did not result in hull losses.[3] The accident rates should be adjusted downward by an applicability factor derived by examining one historic accident at a time and

---

[1]Global data are used because there are (fortunately) insufficient accident data at individual airports. Also, because even in the global data there are small numbers of crash events by aircraft type, it is better from a statistical point of view to aggregate the data somewhat, such as by size of aircraft. For example, although our model can handle as many types as desired, we grouped the aircraft into three types by size—large, medium, and small—and performed the quantitative analysis on these three types. Furthermore, the aircraft-type mix at an airport in the future may not be known with great precision, and therefore it would be misleading to disaggregate the data into more aircraft types.

[2]The sources of the crash and causal data we used are Douglas Aircraft Company, Boeing Commercial Airplane Group, the Civil Aviation Authority of the United Kingdom, and the United Nations' International Civil Aviation Organization (ICAO).

[3]One could envision various possibilities. For example, a cargo door falling off a flying aircraft could kill a person on the ground, but the aircraft lands safely. Such events are so rare that they are insignificant for this study.

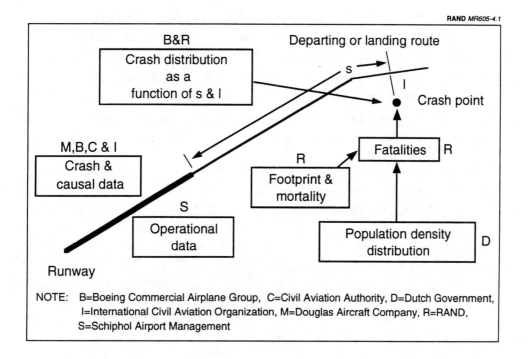

Figure 4.1—Schematic of Data and Data Sources for Risk Estimation

asking the question: Could the accident have occurred in the current environment at this airport? One might remove, for example, some accidents in which aircraft struck mountains when there are no mountains in the vicinity of the airport. On the other hand, it is necessary to keep those accidents that might have occurred even if the mountain were not there. One should also discard other accidents that are clearly inapplicable to the airport under study, such as those caused by civil war when the airport is not now or expected to be in an area subject to such warfare. We also make other adjustments to eliminate accidents that have occurred inside airports or far from the airport (during cruise).[4] We then calculate the expected number of crashes that could contribute to third-party external risk by multiplying the number of movements at the airport by the adjusted accident rate for each particular type of aircraft.

Given the expected number of hull loss crashes, we then represent the distribution of crashes as a function of the longitudinal distance along the intended flight path(s) and the lateral distance from the flight path using crash

---

[4]Only a portion of accidents occur outside but near an airport. We have used the historical data to determine that portion.

36

data defining the x and y location of crashes relative to runway.[5] We next estimate the footprint and mortality factor for each type of aircraft. Finally, population data describing the population density as a function of location relative to the airport (data frequently available from environmental noise studies) are used by the model to show the effects of crashes in specific locations (individual and group risk). These population distribution data should include variations by business and nonbusiness hours.

The SAGE-A model permits, for policy analysis purposes, the determination of risk differentiated by scenario year, aircraft type, time of day, phase of flight, particular flight paths, and size of footprint. Figure 4.2 illustrates this differentiation of the data.

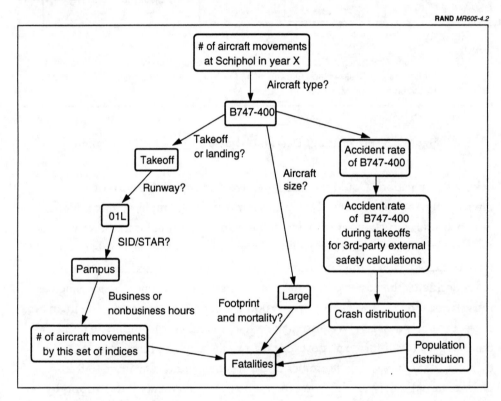

Figure 4.2—Differentiation of Data for Risk Estimation

---

[5]Unfortunately, data regarding intended flight path are not readily available, so it is necessary to approximate the s and l distribution. In our study, we used Boeing data to determine a distribution as a function of distance along the runway centerline (x) and the lateral deviation from it (y). This x/y distribution was used as if it were a s/l distribution. This involves the "bending" of the x/y distribution along SIDs. For a more detailed description, see the discussion of this distribution later in this chapter.

Data Development

The following subsections describe the use of data to create inputs for the SAGE-A model in more detail. We illustrate the development of these data by describing the work done to create a database for a study of the external safety of Schiphol airport in Amsterdam (Hillestad et al., 1993).

Determining Crash Rate at an Airport

Global aircraft crash data over the last 20 to 30 years tell us about the cause or causes of aircraft crashes, crash rates by mode of flight and size of aircraft, impact area, and mortality rate. Using these global data and specific facts about the airport under study (such as geography, weather patterns, and types of aircraft using the airport), we are able to selectively pick and then apply this global information to a specific study of external risk.

The database we have used is derived from multiple sources including the following:

- Airline Pilots Association
- Airport Council International
- Air Transport Association (ATA)
- Aviation Information System Limited (AISL)
- Boeing Commercial Airplane Group
- United Kingdom Civil Aviation Authority (CAA)
- Douglas Aircraft Safety Data Office
- Dutch Aviation Authorities
- Flight Safety Foundation
- KLM pilots
- International Civil Aviation Organization (ICAO)
- Federal Aviation Administration (FAA)
- U.S. National Transportation Safety Board (NTSB)
- Schiphol Airport Authorities
- World Airline Accident Summary (WAAS)
- U.S. National Safety Council (NSC).

The main sources for the loss data were Boeing, Douglas, and the British Civil Aviation Authority. Both aggregate statistics and individual aircraft crash characteristics were assessed and, in some cases, evaluated.

In many instances, Boeing or Douglas had already derived and included aggregate crash data in their accident documents. When this had been done, we borrowed generously from them. In other instances, the data had to be assembled and then derived.

For this analysis, we determined that many of the worldwide aircraft hull loss accidents could have happened at Schiphol had they not happened elsewhere. Thus, safety-enhancement measures that would have mitigated these accidents worldwide would likely reduce the potential for losses at Schiphol.

We exercised care to ensure that we did not reject a crash as being irrelevant to Schiphol merely because the circumstances appeared to differ significantly. For example, and perhaps as the extreme case, we assessed that a crash largely caused by blowing sand (in Africa) could also have occurred at Schiphol because the inducing mechanism was the reduced visibility caused by the sand and not the sand itself. Thus, blowing sand in this instance had the same influence as fog at Schiphol. Many accidents had similar, albeit different, translations in terms of applicability at Schiphol.

Several accidents, however, would likely not have happened at Schiphol, and these were omitted from further consideration. For example, one crash of a U.S. Air Force KC-135 aerial tanker was omitted because it happened on a low-level flyby during an air show and was caused by wake turbulence induced by a B-52 in formation ahead. Because air shows and formation flights are unlikely at Schiphol, this accident was omitted.

Although Schiphol has no nearby high terrain, crashes into high terrain were, in some cases, deemed applicable and others were omitted. This was appropriate because crashes into high terrain can be divided into two classes—those in which an airplane was off course and hit a mountain (but at a correct altitude for the course originally planned), and those in which an airplane crashed because it had incorrect altitude information (because an altimeter was incorrectly set, approach chart altitudes were incorrectly interpreted, etc.).

Of these, the latter was deemed applicable to Schiphol. The rationale for this decision was that, even though Schiphol's surrounding terrain is relatively flat, incorrect altitude information could have caused a crash. Off-course errors would likely not have occurred, however, because there is no high terrain into which to crash near Schiphol, and, thus, we did not consider this category of accident. The result of this step was to provide an accident rate by aircraft type and flight phase.

By weighting these rates by the current number of movements at Schiphol, we obtained the accident rates for the Schiphol fleet composition shown in Table 4.1, but these rates were derived before applying a Schiphol applicability factor, as detailed below. Table 4.2 shows that the weighted overall accident rates, before adjustment by this factor, are 4.5, 1.8, and 1.8 per million departures for the current year, 2003, and 2015, respectively. The lower future rates are due mostly to the expected diversion of 95 percent of general aviation currently at Schiphol to other airports and the trend toward an increasing proportion of larger, presumably safer aircraft at Schiphol.

Table 4.1

**Accident Rates Before Adjustments for the
Current Fleet Composition at Schiphol**

Aircraft Size	Category	No. of Aircraft Movements	Accident Rates (Per Million Departures)	Weighted Total
Large	Com, non-east	48,437	2.26	
	Com, east	1,979	4.52	2.35
Medium	Com, non-east	106,767	1.08	
	Com, east	529	2.15	
	Other com	692	1.08	1.08
Small	Com, non-east	47,849	2.71	
	Com, east	16	5.41	
	Other com	13,990	2.71	
	Non-com	26,326	27.07	9.98
Total		246,585		4.52

NOTE: Com=Commercial, East=Eastern European countries and former Soviet Union, non-com=non-commercial or general aviation.

Table 4.2

**Accident Rates for the Calculation of Third-Party
External Risk at Schiphol**

	Accident Rate (Per Million Departures)		
	Current	2003	2015
Hull loss accidents	4.5	1.8	1.8
Adjusted for Schiphol	3.9	1.5	1.5
Adjusted for third-party external risk	1.3	0.50	0.50
Takeoff accidents	0.32	0.13	0.12
Landing accidents	0.95	0.38	0.37

40

The first adjustment of these rates is to eliminate those accidents that could not have occurred at Schiphol. Studying 114 hull loss accidents between 1987 and 1992 worldwide, we found that 14 percent of those should be excluded, and we arrived at an adjustment factor of 0.86. Consequently, Table 4.2 shows that the rates adjusted by this factor are 3.9, 1.5, and 1.5 per million departures for the current year, 2003, and 2015, respectively. Excluding the 67 percent of accidents that would have occurred inside the airport or far away during the cruise phase (more than 30 km),[6] we arrived at 1.3, 0.5, and 0.5 per million departures for the same three years. These were further divided into rates for takeoffs and landings based on the phase of flight distribution of accidents. For example, the number of takeoff accidents that could result in third-party external risk is 0.32 per million departures for the year 1991, while that of landing accidents is 0.95 per million departures.[7]

Joint Probability of Crash Location

Our model requires a probability distribution for the location of a crash relative to a flight's SID or STAR. This distribution should describe the dispersion of distance from the runway along the SID or STAR and distance, l, perpendicular to the departing or landing route, as depicted in Figure 4.1. The data available to us included all hull loss crashes worldwide since 1 January 1982 for which a crash location was recorded in the Boeing data. The crash sites were measured relative to the centerline of the applicable end of the runway (exiting end for takeoffs, entry end for landing). We used an x-y representation of crash sites, where x is the coordinate of the site parallel to the extended runway centerline and measured from the end of the runway, and y is the coordinate of the site perpendicular to the extended centerline.

The available data presented several problems to us. First, few crashes had site locations: 41 landings and only 12 takeoffs. Second, our model uses locations relative to the SID or STAR, but our data were measured relative to the extended runway centerline. Third, we had locations for only a selected group of crashes, and it was unclear how they were selected. For example, if all crashes within five miles of the airport were measured, but only some crashes outside five miles of the airport were measured, a distortion would be introduced if, of the distant

---

[6]The 30 km is in agreement with the 15 n mi radius within which the landing and departing aircraft are generally considered to be under the approach control of ATC. Moreover, the population data available to us cover an area of about 50.5 by 54 km around Schiphol. This area also corresponds to a radius of about 30 km.

[7]Throughout this section, component numbers sometimes do not sum exactly because of rounding.

crashes, only those nearest the centerline were measured. Fourth, pilot behavior can be presumed to affect the locations of crashes, in particular if pilots attempt to avoid populated areas. It is unclear how this would be reflected in our data and unclear how it would affect the possible location of a new crash near Schiphol. Fifth, the data are coarse: Almost 60 percent of the crashes were measured as being exactly on the extended runway centerline. Finally, as with other data sources we used, the relevance to Schiphol of crashes at other airports is uncertain.

These problems affected several decisions about how to summarize these data and how to represent crash sites in the model. To the extent that we could, we made conservative choices in the sense they tended to disperse the probability, which we judged was an appropriate way to reflect our uncertainty about crash location. The effect of these choices is to diminish the apparent effectiveness of safety measures that involve manipulating runways and SIDs.

The principal feature of our data was its clear bifurcation: 31 of 53 crash sites were clustered on the centerline near the end of the runway, and the 22 crash sites not on the centerline made a highly dispersed pattern in both x and y directions. When all 53 crashes are taken together, the crash sites show increasing dispersion in the y direction as x (distance from the end of the runway) increases, because the centerline crashes tend to be much closer to the end of the runway than the off-centerline crashes.

However, for crashes not on the centerline, there is little if any indication in these data that dispersion in the y direction increases with distance from the end of the runway. The 16 landing crashes off the centerline show no increasing dispersion. The six takeoff crashes off the centerline are consistent with increasing y dispersion as x increases, but with so few points it is folly to make such a judgment.

This finding grated on our intuition: We had expected to see y becoming more dispersed as x increased, from the effect of diverging flight paths. Therefore, we formally compared two competing models:

1. No increasing dispersion: First, flip a biased coin to determine whether the crash is on the centerline or not; with probability 31/53 it is, and with probability 22/53 it is not. If the crash is on the centerline, draw its distance from the end of runway from an exponential distribution with mean about 3.5 miles. If the crash is off the centerline, make independent draws to determine its x and y coordinates. The x coordinate is drawn from a normal distribution with mean and standard deviation about 5 miles, and the y

42

coordinate is drawn from a normal distribution with mean zero (i.e., centered on the runway centerline) and standard deviation about 6 miles. The specific means and variances were estimated from the data, and the distributional forms (exponential and normal) were adequate according to standard diagnostic plots.

2. Increasing dispersion: Draw the y coordinate from a normal distribution with mean 0 and variance $a + b\,x^2$, where a and b are adjustable constants estimated from the data. The x coordinate could be drawn from any of several distributions; we tried a normal distribution and an exponential distribution, with the respective adjustable constants estimated from the data.

Model (1) allows crashes with negative x values (past the end of the runway for landings, before the end of the runway for takeoffs), of which our data contained two, both landings. Model (2) embodies our intuition, in that the dispersal of crash location increases with distance from the end of the runway. It could produce data consistent with ours: As the x distance increases, there are fewer crashes, and thus fewer opportunities to observe extreme draws from the y distribution, so that dispersion might not be apparent. Model (2) does not allow crash sites with negative x values if x is drawn from an exponential distribution.

In the formal comparison, model (1) prevailed, even when we attempted to favor model (2) by changing the distribution in the x direction and by dropping a few crashes that counted most heavily against model (2).

On the basis of these formal tests, we elected to use model (1). Further, we decided to use model (1) to represent crashes relative to SIDs and STARs, although we also ran a case that ignored SIDs and STARs and used model (1) relative to the runway centerline.

The dispersion of the crashes defined by this model, it turns out, is consistent with the intuition of air traffic controllers and others, who expressed the opinion that the pilot of a distressed aircraft will not pay much attention to the planned flight path and may have little control over the aircraft, so that crash sites should show considerable dispersion and little relationship to planned flight paths.

Population Data

In the Schiphol study, the population data were provided to us by Advanced Decision Systems (ADS) at Delft. There are six sets of data representing population distributions in 1991, 2003, and 2015 during business hours and nonbusiness hours. Since ADS did not define business and nonbusiness hours, we classified 8 am to 6 pm during weekdays as business hours. All other hours are nonbusiness. The cell size for each data point is 100 by 100 m, and the overall grid size covers an area centering around Schiphol, 50.5 km in the north-south direction and 54 km in the east-west direction. The actual boundaries within which population data are available are shown in Figures 4.3 and 4.4. Moreover,since the original data came in a much more aggregate scale, the figures in the 100-by-100 m cells are often average values of cell sizes much larger. The primary source of information was Dutch census data in the form of the number of registered houses per municipality or block. Since ADS had to use the same average number of occupants per house across all houses, the derived population distribution is subject to this translation error. ADS

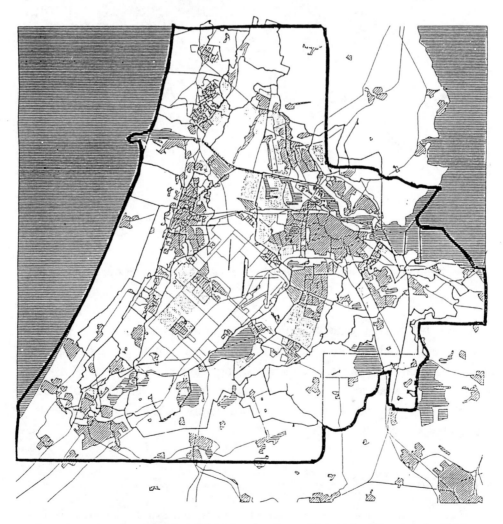

Figure 4.3—Boundary Within Which Housing Data of Municipalities Are Available

Figure 4.4—Boundary Within Which Housing Data Are Available in Addition to Those Provided by Municipalities

supplemented the basic data with information (location, number of beds, students, etc.) about individual hospitals, schools, retirement homes, mental homes, psychiatric centers, and student housing near Schiphol. It also incorporated into the database the distribution of about 517,000 laborers. Finally, ADS provided some data about the types of structures occupied during business and nonbusiness hours.

Operational Data

Listed below are the operational data used in our analysis and model runs but not already described. Table 4.3 shows the sizes of the aircraft types serviced by

Table 4.3

Schiphol Aircraft Sizes and Movements

Aircraft Type	Aircraft Size	Number of Aircraft Movements at Schiphol in 1991[a]
Boeing 747-400	L	5,682
Boeing 747-300/200/100/SP	L	12,089
DC-10-30/40	L	4,327
Tristar L-1011-500/100	L	2,555
Boeing 767	L	3,288
Airbus A-300	L	450
DC-8-60/70/30/50	L	636
Airbus A-310	L	13,499
Boeing 707	L	1,882
Boeing 757	L	4,029
Boeing 727	M	3,060
A-320	M	4,302
MD 80	M	7,192
DC-9-50/40/30/10	M	12,562
Boeing 737-500/400/300	M	42,280
Boeing 737-200	M	16,176
BAE 1-11	M	4,222
BAE 146	M	8,936
Fokker F100	M	1,654
Fokker F28	M	6,383
Other medium commercial aircraft	M	692
Small commercial aircraft	S	47,849
East European countries and FSU		
• An 124, Illyushin 86/76/62, Tu 154	L	1,979
• Illyushin 18, An 12, Tu 134	M	529
• Yak 40	S	16
Other commercial flights	S	13,990
Noncommercial flights	S	26,326
Total		246,585

[a]Derived from Schiphol Airport Authority, *Statistical Annual Review* 1991, pp. 34–38.

Schiphol. Also shown are their aircraft movements in 1991. These data are used to calculate the weighted average of accident rates for large, medium, and small aircraft serviced by Schiphol.

Tables 4.4 to 4.7 describe the distributions of takeoffs and landings by runway and aircraft size. Runway 04/22 is a short runway and suitable for use only by small aircraft, and the same practice will continue for the years 2003 and 2015.

There are two cases for the year 2003. The one with four runways is labeled as 2003.4 and that with five runways as 2003.5.

Tables 4.8 and 4.9 give information about the distribution among various SIDs for takeoffs.

Table 4.4

**Distribution of Takeoffs by Runways in
Percentages: 1991 and 2003.4**

	Aircraft Size		
Runway	Small	Medium	Large
01L	22.3	27.4	27.4
19L	5.0	6.1	6.1
09	7.1	8.8	8.8
24	46.9	57.7	57.7
04	18.7	0	0
01LL	0	0	0
Total	100.0	100.0	100.0

Table 4.5

**Distribution of Takeoffs by Runways in
Percentages: 2015 and 2003.5**

	Aircraft Size		
Runway	Small	Medium	Large
01L	8.1	8.2	8.2
19L	20.4	20.7	20.7
19R	3.4	3.5	3.5
09	2.4	2.4	2.4
24	45.7	46.2	46.2
04	1.1	0	0
27	2.7	2.7	2.7
01LL	16.2	16.4	16.4
Total	100.0	100.1	100.1

Table 4.6

**Distribution of Landings by Runways in
Percentages: 1991 and 2003.4**

Total	Aircraft Size		
Runway	Small	Medium	Large
19R	29.5	33.1	33.1
01R	8.9	10.0	10.0
27	20.1	22.6	22.6
06	30.6	34.3	34.3
22	10.9	0	0
19RR	0	0	0
Total	100.0	100.0	100.0

Table 4.7

**Distribution of Landings by Runways in
Percentages: 2015 and 2003.5**

	Aircraft Size		
Runway	Small	Medium	Large
19R	12.1	12.2	12.2
01R	6.6	6.7	6.7
27	7.4	7.5	7.5
06	17.5	17.7	17.7
22	1.1	0	0
01L	1.1	1.2	1.2
09	.2	.2	.2
24	1.3	1.4	1.4
19RR	52.7	53.3	53.3
Total	100.0	100.2	100.2

Table 4.8

Distribution of Takeoffs by SIDs in Percentages: 1991 and 2003.4

	Runway				
SID	01L	19L	90	24	04[a]
Pampus	10.82				
Pampus Special	20.44				
Lekko	8.62	25.20	25.15	17.94	20.00
Lekko Special	16.43				
Lopik	1.60	4.64	4.61	4.61	
Lopik Special	3.00				
Spykerboor	1.40			4.01	
Spykerboor Special	2.61				
Bergi	15.43	15.42	15.33	9.52	20.00
Bergi Special	17.13			5.81	
Valko	2.51	17.64	14.63	17.54	
Refso/Volla		2.12	4.91	2.10	20.00
Woody				7.21	
Nyke		23.29	23.65	14.63	20.00
Nyke Special				8.92	
Andik		11.69	11.72	4.81	20.00
Andik Special				2.91	

[a]For weekends, add Lopik and assign 16.67 percent to each of six SIDs.

Crash Footprint and Number of Fatalities

Estimating the number of fatalities and injuries on the ground from an aircraft crash is very difficult at best. The variables to consider include:

- Size and weight of the aircraft

- Amount of fuel on board

Table 4.9

Distribution of Takeoffs by SIDs in Percentages:[a]
2015 and 2003.5

SID	Runway							
	01L	19L	19R	09	24	04	27	01LL
Pampus	21.81						10.91	21.81
Pampus Special								
Lekko	21.49	21.49	21.49	21.49	21.49	21.49	21.49	21.49
Lekko Special								
Lopik	5.10	5.10	5.10	5.10	5.10	5.10	5.10	5.10
Lopik Special								
Spykerboor	16.10				8.05		16.10	16.10
Spykerboor Special								
Bergi	15.95	15.95	15.95	15.95	15.95	15.95	15.95	15.95
Bergi Special								
Valko and Falcon	19.55	19.55	19.55	19.55	19.55	19.55	19.55	19.55
Refso/Volla								
Woody								
Nyke		21.81	21.81	21.81	21.81	21.81		
Nyke Special								
Andik		16.10	16.10	16.10	8.05	16.10		
Andik Special								

[a]For weekends, add Lopik and assign 16.67 percent to each of six SIDs.

- Angle of impact of the aircraft with the ground or the structure

- Size and orientation of structure

- Strength of structure

- Combustibility of structure

- Skid path before collision with structure

- Effectiveness of emergency response

- Size of the area hit.

The number of fatalities and injuries on the ground from an aircraft crash can be estimated in two parts: First, calculate *mortality rate given a crash* (M) per 100-by-100 m grid (the probability that there is a fatality in the grid cell assuming there is a crash) and, second, estimate the number of grids affected (*the impact area or* A).

To estimate M, we begin by assuming the condition "there is a crash."

There are few data on M from prior crashes. (Over the last 20 years, there may have been only a few dozen cases of ground mortalities following aircraft crashes, and most have been one to a few score mortalities per crash.) Hence, no one can predict with high certainty the value of M. Several analysts in the past have devised analytic techniques for addressing the value of M.[8]

Although the approaches these analysts took are quite sound analytically, typically their approaches are specific to a hardened structure (nuclear reactor Class 1 buildings, such as the reactor containment) and assume a worst-case impact. Using these approaches as a basis, we can devise a parametric means for determining M. The value of M takes into account the size and weight of the aircraft, the fuel it has on board, and the nature of the structure hit by the aircraft.

Based on the prior studies, limited data on prior accidents, and a heuristic parametric approach, Table 4.10 offers a rule for estimating the percentage of people killed relative to the total number of people in the structure (M or mortality rate given a crash). The value of M varies between 0 and 1.

The "no building assumption" would be valid for residential and smaller (i.e., four or fewer apartments) buildings.

Table 4.10

Mortality Rate Given a Crash

M	Aircraft	Structure
0.90	Large,[a] takeoff	Single family to few-story apt.
0.75	Large, landing	Single family to few-story apt.
0.40	Medium, takeoff	Single family to few-story apt.
0.30	Medium, landing	Single family to few-story apt.
0.20	Small, takeoff	Single family to few-story apt.
0.15	Small, landing	Single family to few-story apt.
0.50	Large, takeoff	Office, high rise apt., theater, etc.
0.40	Large, landing	Office, high rise apt., theater, etc.
0.30	Medium, takeoff	Office, high rise apt., theater, etc.
0.20	Medium, landing	Office, high rise apt., theater, etc.
0.10	Small, takeoff	Office, high rise apt., theater, etc.
0.10	Small, landing	Office, high rise apt., theater, etc.

[a]A reasonable definition of large and small aircraft based on the literature would categorize large as holding more than 30 passengers; all else would be small. If we have three categories (small, medium, and large), those holding fewer than 30 passengers would be considered small; DC10s, L1011s, and B747s would be large; and all others would be medium. These categorizations have been used in the literature to some extent. See, for instance, Wall and Augenstein (1970); Chelapati and Kennedy (1972).

[8]See, for example, Wall and Augenstein (1970), Chelapati and Kennedy (1972), and Kennedy (1966).

To estimate total area when there is a taller building, we must consider three components to the impact area. The first component is the vacant lot area (discussed above); second is the shadow area defined by the impact angle; and third is the skid area, defined as the area immediately in front of the building when an aircraft crashes and skids into the building. The skid area and the shadow area calculations are given in Solomon et al. (1974), Solomon (1975a), Solomon (1975b), and Solomon (1987). As a rule of thumb, for larger buildings, the total impact area (vacant lot, shadow, and skid) could be up to three times that of the vacant lot area that the building occupies. Of course, many larger buildings could be surrounded by parks, open areas, parking lots, and other areas not heavily populated.

The impact area for a vacant lot could also be estimated as in Solomon et al. (1974). For example, the wing span of a B747 is 195 ft. 8 in. The skid distance during a shallow-angle, takeoff crash (based on prior studies of accidents) is up to a half to three-quarters of a mile (say around 3500 feet). Multiplying 3500 ft by 200 ft equals an area of 700,000 square feet or about 0.025 square miles. The value 0.025 square miles affects several 100-by-100 m grids.

Based on prior studies and standards (Wall and Augenstein, 1970; Chelapati and Kennedy, 1966; Kennedy, 1966), the impact area (A) can be estimated for the several conditions assuming an open field, i.e., no buildings (Table 4.11).

For the purpose of the runs made in the Schiphol study, we assumed that the mortality rate is consistent with the single-family dwelling to few-story apartment building version of Table 4.10. We further assumed that the impact

Table 4.11

Impact Area Following a Crash

A (sq mi)	Aircraft	Impact Angle
0.020	Large, takeoff	Steep[a]
0.015	Large, landing	Steep
0.015	Medium, takeoff	Steep
0.010	Medium, land	Steep
0.010	Small, takeoff	Steep
0.005	Small, landing	Steep
0.025	Large, takeoff	Shallow
0.020	Large, landing	Shallow
0.020	Medium, takeoff	Shallow
0.015	Medium, land	Shallow
0.015	Small, takeoff	Shallow
0.010	Small, landing	Shallow

[a]Greater than 20 degrees.

angle (see Table 4.11) is steep. Our model is fully capable of running other mortality and impact area values. Table 4.12 reflects our model inputs for the sets of runs reflected in the present study.

Uncertainties in Data

Aircraft accidents are low-probability events. A typical accident rate is on the order of a few accidents per million flights. Even with a quarter of a million flights a year at busy airports such as Schiphol, there are insufficient accident data to allow a statistical analysis of the current and future safety at that airport to be based solely on data at that airport. Instead, one could use incident data, which are related to near accidents or events that could have potentially led to accidents. These data are much more numerous. Although incidents provide useful information about safety problem areas and the adequacy of responses, these data alone cannot be used to predict accident rates, because one does not know what fraction and types of incidents will turn into accidents. Thus, one is compelled to use accident data at other airports to bolster the number of data points. The probability that a specific type of accident will occur at one airport will generally be different at another. The terrain and the weather conditions may be different, as may be the ability of the ground and air crews in handling unexpected problems and emergencies. The fleet may consist of less–well-maintained aircraft and may be equipped differently. All these factors affect air safety significantly. The applicability of global data to a specific airport is one area of uncertainty.

Another problem area involves the global accident data themselves. First, the Western world knows little about accidents inside the former Soviet Union (FSU) and the Warsaw Pact, especially in the past. Yet we have to deal with the potentially increasing number of Eastern European aircraft flying into Western Europe. Judging by data released by the FSU, the West has reported the dubious

Table 4.12

Impact Area and Mortality Rate Values Used in Our Runs

Size	Impact Area, A (sq mi)		Mortality Rate, M	
	Takeoff/Climb	Landing/Approach	Takeoff/Climb	Landing/Approach
Large	0.020	0.015	0.90	0.75
Medium	0.015	0.010	0.40	0.30
Small	0.010	0.005	0.20	0.15

result that Eastern aircraft are as safe as, or even safer than, Western counterparts.[9] On the other hand, a recent analysis indicates that the accident rate of controlled flights into terrain (CFIT) by jet transport aircraft in the Eastern Bloc countries during 1959 through 1991 was 6.6 times as high as that in Europe (Boeing Aircraft, 1991). Second, even when we know the accidents occurred, we still lack detailed information about some of them. The West knows very little about accidents taking place in the Third World, either because accident investigation is not performed or the reports are not available to the West.

The third area deals with nonaccident data. Accident rates are derived by dividing the number of accidents by the number of departures, flight hours, air miles, or some other operational proxy. The number of accidents (the numerator) is widely available, but accident rates are found only in very aggregate forms, such as number of accidents per million departures. Accident rates based on other denominators—namely, those characterizing specific conditions of flights—are much more difficult to find. For the Schiphol study, accident rates by aircraft type have been provided by Douglas Aircraft Company.[10] Other rates, such as those based on weather severity, time of day, and terrain, are unavailable. The paucity of such rates has little to do with accident data, but much to do with nonaccident data. The accident investigation reports by NTSB give detailed information about the accidents, the surrounding environment, and the likely causes. This permits classification of accidents according to various conditions of interest. Lacking, however, are sufficient nonaccident data: how many flights were successful through severe weather, at night, over mountains, and so on. Without this denominator, it is difficult to estimate the effects of avoidance measures, such as restricting flight under adverse weather conditions. There is also little information about accident rates under combined conditions, such as the rate under low visibility *and* at night. Fortunately, this "denominator problem" does not preclude us from using Bayesian techniques to examine the effects of safety-improvement options. The use of an automatic landing system (for instance, coupled approaches) during low visibility—if not creating additional problems of its own—would be such a safety option, by virtue of its ability to compensate for loss of visibility. Thus, one can reduce or eliminate the

---

[9]For example, using data released by the State Supervisory Commission for Flight Safety (Gosavianadzor), Council of Ministers, FSU, Shung C. Huang reported that the fatal accidents per 100,000 flight hours for FSU and the member states of the International Civil Aviation Organization (shown in parentheses) during 1981-1985, 1986, 1987, 1988, and 1989 were 0.09 (0.14), 0.12 (0.09), 0.05 (0.12), 0.08 (0.12), and 0.03 (0.14), respectively. These figures, if valid, would have indicated that the FSU aircraft were safer. ("Worldwide Airline Fatal Accidents and Jet Transport Aircraft Hull Losses," 1991, p. 20.) On the other hand, ICAO reported that FSU flights had similar rates under a different measure. During 1986, 1987, and 1988, the passenger fatalities per 100 million passenger-kilometers for scheduled services including and excluding (in parentheses) the FSU flights were 0.04 (0.03), 0.06 (0.06), and 0.04 (0.05), respectively. ICAO, 1988, p. 11.

[10]Some of the same data also appear in Douglas Aircraft (1991), p. 15.

rate of accidents under such conditions without explicit knowledge of—or adjustment of—the denominator.

The fourth area deals with crash distribution data. Given that a crash will occur, one still has to determine where the aircraft will actually crash. Traditionally, one gets an idea by plotting crash locations with respect to the centerline of the runway from which the troubled aircraft took off or on which it was intended to land. One then models the crash distribution as a function of longitudinal distance along the centerline and the lateral distance from it. A more appropriate reference path could be the intended route of the aircraft or, as an approximation, the SID or STAR, if one is used. Accident investigation reports might record the name or the number of the SID or STAR used by the crashed aircraft, but the route is not graphically displayed in the reports. We know of no one who has compiled and published in one document the routes and crash locations of aircraft accidents. Neither did we have the time to search old records at airports for the SID or STAR at the time of the accident. Determination of the crash distribution is further complicated by the fact that the actual path for even a trouble-free flight often deviates considerably from the SID. An aircraft in distress is more unlikely to follow a SID. All these factors make the crash location distribution highly uncertain.

The fifth area deals with crash footprint and mortality. Even when the crash location is known, one needs to determine the impact damage area or footprint, which is affected by the size of the aircraft, the angle of impact, and the obstacles and types of structure/vegetation on the ground. The angle of impact may not be known if no one survives the crash, if the flight recorder is not recovered or usable, or if there is no ground observer. The problem, however, is not so much a lack of information as lack of a model to correlate footprint size with the combined effect of these parameters and lack of a database to describe the structures, topology, and other features around the airport, which are relevant to predicting footprint sizes of crashes around the airport. Similarly, the percentage of inhabitants within the footprint who will be killed is also hard to ascertain, even if one knows the fuel load of the aircraft, the combustibility of the ground structure, and all other pertinent information.

The implication of these uncertainties is that a model to predict risk should be used cautiously, and the predictions of individual or group risk should not be taken as definitive. Rather, the model should be used to indicate the direction of improvement or degradation in safety that might be taken when a change to airport operations or its environment that might affect safety is proposed or implemented. It might also be used to compare the relative magnitude of external risk change across several changes.   Even in these cases it is important not to ignore the uncertainties in prediction and for this reason *the SAGE-A model produces estimates of the uncertainty of any prediction of individual or group risk.*

5. Policy Applications of the Sage-A Model

SAGE-A is designed for the analysis of policies that affect the external safety of
airports. It permits inputs representing policies that affect the crash risk of the
mix of aircraft using the airport, such as restricting activities of certain risky
carriers or aircraft types. Takeoff and landing patterns, runway configuration
zoning, and various types of crash barriers also affect crash risk and mortality.
We list here some of the options that can be studied with this model.

Policy Options That Affect Crash Risk

These options relate to the prediction of the probability of a crash and not
necessarily its location or the effect of the crash on the surrounding population.

- Changing the mix of aircraft
  - Restricting particular carriers from using the airport
  - Permitting new aircraft types or carriers to use the airport (if they have
    no safety record, the safety record of an equivalent type may have to be
    used; however, if they are larger, for example, other factors, such as
    crash footprint, would be affected)
  - Restricting certain types of aircraft from using the airport or particular
    runways (e.g., restricting general aviation)
  - Accounting for safety improvements in aircraft or ATC technology (if,
    for example, certain types of aircraft were retrofitted with new and
    safer communication technology, they would then be represented by an
    accident rate reflective of the pool of aircraft with this technology)

- Changing the operations rate at the airport (this is a multiplier of the single-
  flight crash rate that determines the cumulative crash risk)
  - Allowing more takeoffs and landings because of airport growth or
    increased demand
  - Increasing or reducing the number of flight operations by aircraft type
    because of load factor increases, consolidation of carriers, adding new
    carriers, etc.

- Changing the crash rate of specific aircraft types or carriers

- — Accounting for future safety improvements in training, technology, inspections, etc., if the effects on crash rate can be predicted
- — Increasing the crash rates of aircraft types or carriers that have been shown to have a higher crash risk than is reflected in the historical data

- Changing the general risk of crash near an airport (these options make the airport generally safer with respect to crash risk. They can be accommodated in the model by reducing the crash risk by that portion of historical accidents that would no longer occur.)
  - — Stricter bird and wildlife control
  - — Deicing procedures
  - — Changing VFR and IFR procedures
  - — Airport closure policies for weather
  - — Wind shear sensors
  - — General maintenance, loading, and dispatching procedures
  - — Restricting potential flight interference from other aircraft (e.g., general aviation and helicopters)
  - — Improvements in ATC and communication.

Policy Options That Affect Crash Location and Individual Risk

These options do not generally affect the frequency of crash but change the ground locations at which crashes occur and the region over which the mortality effects of a crash are experienced. These same options affect the individual risk in a particular location. Of course, the individual risk is also affected by the previous options that determine the crash risk. Some of the important policy options include:

- Adding runways to an airport

- Changing the use of existing runways

- Adding, deleting, or changing departure and arrival routes

- Designating emergency runways, routes, fuel dumping areas, or alternate emergency airports

- Reducing the crash footprint by adding natural or manmade barriers and the use of fire retardants or fire suppression

- Making buildings more fire resistant or structurally stronger

- Improving emergency response to mitigate the effects of a crash.

Policy Options That Affect Group or Societal Risk

These options affect the number of people killed in a crash. The options that affect the probability of a crash and the probability that the crash occurs in a specific location with a specific footprint also affect this risk and have been stated above. However, there are additional policies that can change the group risk. These policies affect the population distribution in the region near the airport and its mortality rate:

- Establishing exclusionary zoning for safety or noise to reduce the number of people in the high-risk zone

- Restricting population and business density to reduce the population in the riskier zones, perhaps during periods of increased flight operations

- Moving or locating an airport away from regions of high population density, as a complement to the above options

- Location of surface transport corridors away from high crash risk areas or putting them underground

- Restricting times of flight operations to limit flights over areas with high day or nighttime populations during the period when the population density is high

- Restricting flights near high temporary concentrations of people, such as stadiums during sporting or other events

- Restricting flights near other facilities with potential high societal risk, such as nuclear generation plants.

Most of these policy options can be rather easily measured in terms of effect on external risk of an airport by changing inputs to the SAGE-A model and comparing them with a baseline risk estimation. Even policies with highly uncertain effects can sometimes be analyzed using *a fortiori* analysis. Suppose it is desired to evaluate an option that is expected to increase external risk. If one makes rather extreme assumptions about the impact of a policy alternative on the input parameters of the model and the resulting effects on individual and group risk are not large, then using more realistic numbers for the policy parameters will not lead to a larger impact.

References

Barnett, Arnold, and May K. Higgins, "Airline Safety: The Last Decade," *Management Science*, Vol. 35, No. 1, January 1989.

Boeing Aircraft, Commercial Airplane Group, *Statistical Summary of Commercial Jet Aircraft Accidents, Worldwide Operations, 1959–1991*, Seattle, Wash., 1991.

Chelapati, C. V., and R. P. Kennedy, "Probabilistic Assessment of Aircraft Hazard for Nuclear Power Plants," *Nuclear Engineering and Design*, Vol. 19, 1972, pp. 333–364.

Douglas Aircraft, Safety Data Office, Flight Standards and Safety Group, *Commercial Jet Transport Safety Statistics*, Long Beach, Calif., 1991.

European Commission, *The LOTOS Study: A View of Future of Civil Aeronautics*, 1991.

Hillestad, Richard, et al., *Airport Growth and Safety: A Study of the External Risks of Schiphol Airport and Possible Safety Enhancement Measures*, Santa Monica, Calif.: RAND, MR-288-EAC/VW, 1993.

ICAO, "Civil Aviation Statistics of the World," *ICAO Statistical Yearbook*, 1988, p. 11.

Kennedy, R. P., *Effects of Aircraft Crashes on Concrete Buildings*, Holmes and Narver, Los Angeles, Calif., July 1966.

"Premises for Risk Management," *Dutch National Environmental Policy Plan*, Second Chamber of the States General Session 1988-1989, Vol. 21, No. 5, 1989.

Solomon, Kenneth A., "Airplane Crash Model," *Journal of Hazard Prevention*, Vol. 11, No. 5, May/June 1975.

Solomon, Kenneth A., "Analyses of Ground Hazards Due to Aircraft and Missiles," *Journal of Hazard Prevention*, Vol. 12, No. 4, March/April 1975.

Solomon, Kenneth A., et al., *Airplane Crash Risk to Ground Populations*, University of California, Los Angeles, UCLA-ENGR-7424, March 1974.

Solomon, Kenneth A., *Ground Risks Associated with Aircraft Crashes*, Santa Monica, Calif.: RAND, P-7459, 1987.

Wall, I. B., and R. C. Augenstein, "Probabilistic Assessment of Aircraft Hazards to Nuclear Power Plants," *Trans. of the American Nuclear Society*, Vol. 13, 1970, p. 217.

"Worldwide Airline Fatal Accidents and Jet Transport Aircraft Hull Losses," *Flight Safety Digest*, February 1991, p. 20.